SAVING THE
FRAGMENTS

SAVING THE FRAGMENTS

From Auschwitz to New York

by
Isabella Leitner
with
Irving A. Leitner

with an Introduction by
Howard Fast

NAL BOOKS

NEW AMERICAN LIBRARY

NEW YORK AND SCARBOROUGH, ONTARIO

NAL BOOKS TRADEMARK REG. U.S. PAT. OFF. AND FOREIGN COUNTRIES
REGISTERED TRADEMARK—MARCA REGISTRADA
HECHO EN HARRISONBURG, VA., U.S.A.

SIGNET, SIGNET CLASSIC, MENTOR, PLUME, MERIDIAN
and NAL BOOKS are published *in the United States* by
New American Library,
1633 Broadway, New York, New York 10019,
in Canada by The New American Library of Canada Limited,
81 Mack Avenue, Scarborough, Ontario M1L 1M8

Library of Congress Cataloging in Publication Data

Leitner, Isabella.
   Saving the fragments.

   1. Leitner, Isabella.   2. Holocaust survivors—
United States—Biography.   3. Jews—United States—
Biography.   I. Leitner, Irving A.   II. Title.
E184.J5L5723 1985   940.53'15'03924   85-8815

Designed by Sherry Brown
First Printing, October, 1985
1 2 3 4 5 6 7 8 9
PRINTED IN THE UNITED STATES OF AMERICA

For Tobe, Mendel, Sadie, Hyman,
Cipi, and Potyo

The sun made a desperate effort to shine on the last day of May in 1944. The sun is warm in May. It heals. But even the heavens were helpless on that day. A force so evil ruled heaven and earth that it altered the natural order of the universe, and the heart of my mother was floating in the smoke-filled sky of Auschwitz. I have tried to rub the smoke out of my vision for forty years now, but my eyes are still burning, Mother.

Introduction
by Howard Fast

Both Isabella Leitner and I have spent all of our lives in the twentieth century. Since I am somewhat older than Mrs. Leitner, my life touches World War I, and it can be said that in all the history of the planet Earth, there has been no period so mindlessly cruel as this twentieth century, so devastating in its disregard for human life and for every symbol of morality that man has painfully acquired through the ages. World Wars I and II took more lives than all the wars preceding them in four thousand years of recorded history. Such acts as the Holocaust, the bombing of Hiroshima and Nagasaki, and the avalanche of death loosed in Vietnam, were matched by lesser but no less monstrous acts—for example, the hundred thousand or more put to death by Idi Amin, the forty thousand victims of the death squads in El Salvador, over a million men, women, and children cut down by the lunatic death squads of Indonesia, the endless murders of both body and soul in South Africa—and currently the murderous religious mania of the Ayatollah Khomeini.

One could go on and on, filling page after page with the infamies indulged in by our so-called modern civilization; nor could one contend that such practices of the twentieth century are confined to the more backward nations of the earth. Hardly the case: the West has indeed taught the more backward nations this manner of "civilization." Most of the showy technical achievements of this century rest on a solid basis of death, and a new generation is currently being taught by TV screens and computers that mercy and compassion are as antiquated as the horse and buggy, and that even the extinction of the human race is permissible.

Where, then, against this depressing background, does an Isabella Leitner fit in? To me, her very existence is an affirmation of life, a song of hope, a clear bright flame that defies the murderers of mankind. She is the antithesis of all the hatred and destruction that we have lived through.

Above all, Mrs. Leitner is an innocent. And what exactly is an innocent? Above all and quite naturally, an innocent is one untouched by guilt. An innocent is one uncorrupted by malice, evil, or hatred, one who is without guile and who seeks to harm no other. A young girl, most fittingly described by the above definition, was taken from her home by a brutal aggressor, thrust into a concentration camp under the power of the unspeakable Dr. Mengele, exposed to horrors that words cannot describe, tortured, used, and starved. She was fortunate enough to survive.

But the fact that Isabella Leitner survived is the lesser part of her personal miracle; the greater part is that she survived—not as a destroyed soul, not as a person utterly crushed by suffering, but as a wonderful, open woman whose delight in life is so pure and enchanting that it becomes a song of victory over the mindless, the hate-filled, and the destroyers.

There have been many other books about the Holocaust, books that attempted to put into words the unthinkable, to define, explain, or bear witness to a crime unequaled in all the history of the human race. This is as it should be. As long as mankind exists, the Holocaust must be remembered, and every attempt to define it and recall it should be cherished, no matter how painful.

But in this litany, Mrs. Leitner has created something unique, the memory of an innocent who, among all that is awful, managed to find, wherever she turned, acts of love. So is mankind redeemed. So am I deeply in debt to Mrs. Leitner, for without these acts of love, hope would be impossible.

This little book is a fragment—as memories are fragments. Isabella Leitner does not attempt to analyze, to explain, to create historical patterns. She cannot; she was a young girl, beloved and innocent, and all she sees and remembers is recalled through the eyes of a young girl.

But the innocence is not without a knife-like edge of wisdom. To be innocent and foolish would prove nothing and teach nothing. To be innocent and naive would negate the validity of responses, but to be cynical would destroy innocence. When, after her hideous experience, Isabella's father asks her to pray to God, she rejects this. She has found in man something truer than the myth of a personal god who savors the smell of burning flesh for reasons beyond our understanding. If there is a God for Isabella, it is something far beyond her father's understanding, something defined only by love and compassion and tied entirely into the lives of men and women who are not Nazis. This is her wisdom.

You do not define or judge the human race by the Nazis. People remain people, and there is something lovely and tender in her comprehension of people and their needs.

The liberating Russian soldiers are people. They have acts of kindness and compassion, yet so long without women, they are ready to grab anyone in a skirt, child or adult—and in the next breath Isabella remembers the wonderful Russian woman on the train, her great bubbling pot of food, and her need to feed anyone who is hungry. She loves all who love. This is her path back into the arms of the human race, and the medley of people of all races who fought and were victimized by the Nazis yet survived fills her with endless delight. Only the Nazi is separate in her mind. For him, there is neither pity nor any shred of tolerance; he must be remembered for all time as the face of evil.

So go with Isabella on this fragmented, life-giving journey of hers, from the time the Russians liberated her and her companions to her arrival in a new world. Even as it took her from the horrors of the crematorium into freedom, it will take you, the reader, into a new place of compassion. These fragments are a preachment, a sermon on the wonder and goodness and value of life. All is possible if men and women deal in trust and love. With hatred and suspicion, all will perish. This is the essence and teaching of Isabella's fragments of memory.

Part One

Liberation

i

It is January 1945. Auschwitz and Birnbaumel are behind us. The advancing Russians have taken Jagadschutz, the village in which we have been hiding since our escape from the Nazi death march to Bergen-Belsen.

Chicha, Rachel, and I are running barefoot through the snow to greet the Red Army. Our shrieks must be heard on planets beyond Earth.

Our shaved heads tell them who we are. A Russian soldier rips the dog tag with my prison number, 79212, off my neck. "You don't need this anymore. You are free!" His words are in Russian, which I don't understand, but his meaning is clear.

The tough Red Army men are good-hearted and compassionate. They give us apples and bread, whatever food they have.

Some time later, however, when pounds have begun to

stick to our bodies, some of the soldiers, drunk and lustful, begin to see us as women; and virginal young girls that we are, we try to save ourselves by fleeing through house windows, hiding in closets, or crawling under beds.

I pull a sock, full of holes, over my hairless head, distort my face to give it an imbecilic look, and walk as though crippled. I am not ready to be raped, even by my saviors, and somehow each time, I escape having to taste first love through foul breath in a desperate land of cruelty and war.

My sisters, Chicha and Rachel, also manage to save themselves. By now we have discovered that there were thirty girls who escaped in our vicinity. But no one has seen Cipi, our fourth sister.

Little Rozi, a Hungarian girl, was raped. She thinks she is pregnant. She walks with a crazed, dazed look on her face. We comfort her without really being able to help.

Three other escapees, our "partners," are Polish. They are able to communicate with the Russian officers and become their lovers. They seem to be knowing, experienced women. They tell me and my sisters that they are shielding us with their own bodies. They begin to order us about, making us clean the deserted house we have "appropriated." They make us cook while they wait for their warring heroes, who visit them whenever they can get back from the fierce battles raging around Breslau. Our Polish friends become our pseudo-slavemasters.

The house is crowded with lovers. Chicha, Rachel, and I still "live" here, but many a night we sleep in another deserted house across the road. A middle-aged woman, who survived with her daughter, is with us in the other house as well.

One night the woman places her daughter on a cot in the anteroom, covers her with layers of down-filled comforters, and lies down on top of her. It is one of those ugly times when drunken heroes seem to be everywhere. I am ill with fever, wearing nothing but a very short blue-and-white cotton something and lying in the same bed with my sister Rachel. The dying flame of a tiny chunk of candle provides the sole illumination.

Two drunken soldiers suddenly charge into our room. They ignore the older woman and her hidden daughter in the anteroom and blow out the struggling, expiring candle. Barefoot, Rachel and I run out of the house and across the snow-covered stretch that leads to our headquarters house, where the officers and the three Polish girls are making love to the sounds of cannon nearby. We know our friends will protect us.

The frustrated soldiers, our would-be lovers, follow us into the white-blanketed night and fire their guns in the air.

Inside our original home, one of the Russian officers speaks to us. He speaks Yiddish to me and, for special comfort, tucks me into bed between him and his Polish girlfriend. As I fall into a weary sleep I am aware of my bedmates changing places in order to love away the night.

ii

The fighting near Breslau is fierce, but our area is clear of the enemy. The Russians in Jagadschutz are now trying to "govern." The fleeing Germans had abandoned their old, their sick, and their livestock. The Russians assign the liberated concentration camp women to cattle duty.

Every day we are forced to feed and clean the cows. The necessity is clear, but we are reluctant to care for the animals. Every morning the Russians have to root us out from our hiding places. We are not cooperative. We have to be forced to work with cud and dung. We know nothing of cattledom, are exhausted from prisondom. We are tired and spent. We want to be cared for ourselves, not made to care for anything or anyone. We are totally unreasonable.

Bloody uniforms are brought back from the front to be washed. Each of us is assigned to wash sixty shirts in lye.

We cry. The lye, mixed with salty tears, is brutal on our hands. Liberation is unreasonable. We feel sorry for ourselves.

We realize that we are the only nonmilitary labor pool available to the Russians. Still, we are resentful. The Russians are good to us. They slaughter a cow and feed us on its flesh. We get huge amounts of meat. Still, there is no bread. There are no operating bakeries, no stores.

We loot in the nearby town of Prauschnitz. I don't know why, but we call it "organizing." Rachel is organizing daily. The mother hen shops and shops for her brood.

Nothing is real, neither our restricted freedom nor our riches. We block Auschwitz from our minds and relish the evolving new era of chaotic order.

Where is our sister Cipi?

iii

As more and more areas in eastern Germany are liberated, the roads begin to yield survivors making their way on foot toward a railroad rumored to be in a town believed to be called Oelsk. Our village of Jagadschutz comes to life.

Hundreds of death-defiers begin to appear on the road. Isn't it strange? After all they have seen, lived through, suffered, known—they do not seem broken. They feed on insane kinds of hopes. So do we.

"Where do you come from?"

"Are you Hungarian? Polish? Italian?"

"Which camp were you in? For how long?"

"Did you escape, or was the camp liberated?"

"How many of your family survived?"

They march, and we shout questions at them. They keep shouting back.

9

"Did you know the Kleins from Kisvarda? The Weisses from Miskolc? The Roths from Nyiregyhaza? The Halperts from Hajdunanas?"

Names and descriptions fill the air. Hope is shouting everywhere.

"Have you seen Rosa or Sarah from Ajak?"

"Have you seen our sister Cipi?"

"How long have you been walking, marching?"

"Where are you going, and why?"

"Everybody is dead."

"No. No. No. My cousin found her sister yesterday. They say my uncle is alive. Rivka's cousin is supposed to be alive somewhere. Somebody heard it from somebody else, just yesterday."

The questions from us to the marchers, the questions from them to us, are irrepressible, constant. The marching language of hope is the sound of a new kind of after-liberation symphony rising from the ashes of the Jews. There were seven in the Katz family, nine in the Gottesman, twelve in the Weisy. How many survived?

The refusal to accept the murder of our families, even after the stench of burning flesh that we know so well, and that stubborn smell of life on the road cannot be explained by anyone.

Who has had training enough in the humanities, in the mind-healing professions, in the emotional, philosophical, and literary terrain to be able to understand this mysterious insistence on life? Either the inward gazes, the depressed faces, and the dragging bodies are not too many, or we do not want to see them. Our eyes are stubborn. They search for life only. Intermittently there is a shriek because someone is told of someone's survival, because we recognize someone or because we ourselves are recognized.

There is nothing inconsequential about the chaos that Hitler has wrought on these roads. It all deals with life, with death, with emotions, with love, with anxiety. Nothing is unmarred by what Hitler did; yet the mystery of humankind resurfacing seemingly unmarred cannot be fathomed. It is almost all there—feelings we used to have, curiosity about everything, love that we can feel, genuine kindness.

Can it all be true, or are we merely taking a hiatus from all that hate we were forced to endure, and coldness will seep into our hearts not long from now?

God, don't let that happen. This warm shower inside feels good, God. Let us be for a while, let us feel good for a bit. We are tired, God. Living in hate was very hard. Do you hear me, God? Living in hate was very hard.

There is a loving relationship between the road people and us. There is some possibility that maybe someone else in our family is alive. Every day, after our morning's cow work, Chicha, Rachel, and I run to the road that draws us to it like a magnet of hope. We must find Philip, our brother. Philip, dear Philip, are you still alive?

Where is Cipi, our sister?

iv

From time to time it dawns on us that we have been detached from the rest of humankind. We will have to relearn how to live, how to hold a fork, how to live with the family of man. Too great a task. The resources within us will have to stand up to a nearly impossible struggle.

We have reverence for life, or no reverence at all. We have flare-ups of hope, or are dead within. We know almost everything about life or death. Still, we have to relearn how to walk, step by painfully fragile step. What will, what can, prop us up through these delicate inner negotiations?

A warring land is not without its share of decomposing bodies. They are strewn all around us. We step over them, devoid of any emotion. Where have we become so hardened? In Auschwitz. All that burning of our mothers, our children, our kin of every shape, gender, and age—all that was only one aspect of the Auschwitz aberration. There were many other sides.

One: the daily removal of the night's dead from the *Blocks* (barracks). Corpses piled high in front of each *Block* every morning, waiting for the *Totekommando* (death squad) to slap them onto their wagons to convey them to the almighty crematorium. There were so many of these emaciated skeletons greeting the morning dew, sun, or rain daily that we no longer had a tear left to shed from our ducts, not even a flutter, just a tiny flutter, to beat in our hearts. Everything inside us had been used up over and over again. We could no longer locate the mourning niche for the dead in our shriveled souls.

We would perk up only if some rags on the dead could be stolen, if something on the bodies was better than what we, the "living," were wearing. It hardened us so, these bodies that were more touchable, more immediate than the burning stench of thousands floating in the sky.

There, but for the grace of each deadly night, was I. It was good to see that my body was missing each morning from the pile of corpses in front of *Block* 2, *Block* 13, *Block* 9.

Our training ground was Auschwitz. It is easy to step over the bodies on the roads of murder country. It is even easier when the bodies are clad in Nazi uniforms. Yet, whatever a body wears, parts of us are dead, and for moments we hurt from our inability to retrieve the heart or hurt of yesteryear. We want to cry not for the dead but for what is dead in us.

Will what we were return? A silent prayer is etched into our footsteps as we heartlessly step over a decomposing arm, a hip, or a head. Hitler's imprint is on the roads, in the sky, everywhere. He tore our insides into unbearable memories. He also set us up for hopes we should not have.

We try not to remember. We try not to think. Hitler, Hitler, why didn't you let us have normal deaths? Funerals? Tears? Why did you set us apart? Just graves, Hitler—we have survived into an age where a grave is a mark of humanity.

When we were growing up, our mothers and teachers taught us other values. The inspirations we were nurtured on were examples of humaneness. We read and wrote poetry of heroism, learned of a common goal for common man, of justice, of being in the service of common good, of becoming healers—doctors, nurses.

Our songs were love songs. We knew and felt tenderness. Were we misled by all who had a share in shaping us into young women and men? Is this the age of mockery, or were the years that sculpted us the mockery?

Hitler, we will forgive nothing you wrought. Even before you murdered us you tried to cripple our minds. We, the people of the Book, had to endure your book burnings. Knowledge in flames.

Some of us will forever weep for the books and schooling you denied us. The broken wings of our minds will always curse you for that. I curse you. So do Sally, Philip, Berta, Sam, Morris, Helen, Edith, Harry, Jacob, Nathan. . . .

There is no peace on the roads, no peace in our hearts. Marchers, where are you marching? Step out of this age. Step off this planet. Life is tainted too much. Auschwitz is even bigger and more than whatever transpired before.

How will the world heal itself of Auschwitz? Is there a large pill for a large virus called hate? Is the world terminal?

Can it get well? Can shattered lives ever be mended? Will saving the fragments be an impossible task?

All these unanswerable ponderings are floating about within our exhausted minds. They are not questions properly formed. They just take up chaotic residence within our souls.

$\mathcal{V}$

Our eyes are fixed on the road. We are desperately trying to refuel our sorrows with hope, baseless hope, but we are so desperate. How else can we hang on and clear our nostrils of that vile stench? We hug and hope anew when a lone voice yells out, "I am from Kisvarda. I had ten sisters and brothers. Parents, too. I am alone."

Chicha, Rachel, and I were born in Kisvarda. We weep, and the lone one marches along.

The sun begins to fade on the cold afternoon. The marchers are fewer. The sun will rise in the morning on a denser group of hopers. Our feelings are sad and glad as we make our way back to the tending of the cows.

We still have to guard against rape but no longer so fiercely. A more permanent core of Russian military personnel is now in place. We do not fear them. It is the movement of forces that is more threatening, but there is less of

17

that now. The armed struggle to defeat the dying beast of Nazidom is farther and farther away from our temporary home.

We begin to accept the fact that we are the guardians of the cattle, that they would suffer hunger were we not to feed them. We cannot let that happen. We know about hunger. The odor of dung and hay is mixed now with the scent of burning flesh in our nostrils. The scent is better this way, more tolerable.

The bloody uniforms are no longer being brought back from the front. Our lives are better, and the road keeps pulling us with hope. It probably is wrong to hope this fervently, but what is there to do? We fantasize that tomorrow, the day after, or soon, Cipi will scream on the road, "Philip, look. Here they are!"

Yesterday passes, tomorrow passes, and soon passes, but the road refuses to yield the precious pair. Cipi and Philip must know that we are standing vigil on the road. Cipi, hurry. Philip, where are you?

Suddenly the road changes its look and its soul. We are riveted with frozen emotions. For the first time in all the years of war and venom, the victims, the vanquished, and the victors are together.

The Russians are leading an enormous number of captured German soldiers down the same road that conveyed the tortured ones, the dear ones, only yesterday. The footprints of love and hate are commingled in the dust, on the cement. This is the first time that we are facing the Nazis from a position of advantage. We are free and they are prisoners. A defeated body of killers, worn and bedraggled, is playing havoc with our tortured hearts.

What shall we do with them? Spit at them? Shout obscenities? Wish death on their children? Tell them that we would love to fill the sky with the smoke of burning flesh—theirs, and their mothers and infants, and their grandmothers and cousins, and their wives and friends, until they number six million?

What are we to do with all that is pent-up in our mending bodies, with our hideously altered memories, with the apocalypse in our heads, with all the pain of our motherlessness? What are we to do now that we can begin to take revenge?

We are stunned with all that has crashed down on us on the road. We are unprepared. We don't know how to handle this good fortune that has suddenly come our way.

We look at each other with ambivalence at this decisive moment of truth. We know that something must appease the deep yearning for vengeance that has festered for so long in our hearts. Rocks to smash their Nazi heads, to splash the cells of their sick minds on the uniforms they were so proud to wear? We must do something, even if the Russians will punish us for it.

But, then, it must be awful to kill. We have never killed before. We are paralyzed simply by contemplating the thought. We are unable to do it. Yet we must do something with our hate. We simply must.

We stoop to the roadbed, pick up some tiny pebbles, and toss the pebbles at the Nazis.

vi

Our killer instinct subsides. We return to the road the following day to look for life.

The liberated keep walking, surging ahead toward the phantom train that will chug them home, where they stubbornly hope to find the missing members of their families. Some days, the crowds are thin; some days, massive.

We keep shouting, "Wherever you come from, have you seen our sister Cipi anywhere? Our brother's name is Philip. Philip Katz. Do you know if he is alive? Have you seen Cipi? Have you seen Philip? Do you know anyone who has? If you see them anywhere, tell them we are alive."

The road is fickle. It keeps betraying us. We are losing hope, but will not give up our dream of finding our sister and brother. We end our frustrating day by walking to a nearby deserted castle, which is frequently used by Red Army troops for overnight bivouac.

The castle ceilings are high enough to touch the heavens. The grand piano is covered with human feces. The bloody brown feathers of a freshly killed chicken decorate the keyboard. Revenge, apparently, can take any form.

We go to the castle for our "shopping" sprees. Looted as it is, the structure still yields wondrous things. One storage room contains built-in closets from floor to ceiling. Each closet is stocked with light bulbs of different sizes.

We need only one bulb but take an armful. Greed and revenge—neither will bring back our family, nor will it make the returning barons at war's end scrounge for bulbs. Still, it is good to know that there is shit on their piano. Let them smell the foul aroma while they listen to the music of that foul, anti-Semitic genius, Richard Wagner.

We don't move into the castle. We need no castles. We return to our original little home that was deserted by the German blacksmith who once lived there and chat with the three Polish girls about their love lives in our tiny palace of lust. We three Hungarian sisters and the Polish girls really belong to each other, for we are separated only in the knowing ways of sex. Our hearts and bodies were bruised by the same calamity. We sought freedom together, so we belong together.

We have been free for several weeks now. With the war farther and farther away from us, our inner chaos subsides somewhat. At intervals there is a modicum of peace in our heads. We are grateful for the ebbing rumblings.

We are settled into a curious routine, but just as we are beginning to feel a sense of stability, our anxiety returns. The cows, which we have resented and learned to care for, are suddenly to be taken away from us.

Everything, it seems, is constantly being taken from us.

The cattle are the only valuable commodity worth transporting anywhere. Where? To Russia? To milk them for the hungry children of that war-ravaged land? We don't know. We are ordered simply to get the cows to a collection point some distance from the barn and to do it immediately.

Inexperienced cowherds that we are, we begin to drive the cattle forward, using long wooden sticks as prods. We know absolutely nothing about the way such a task can be accomplished. We speak no cattle tongue and know no gestures that are intelligible to cows. Despite all our inane commands, the cattle go where they wish.

If we succeed in leading two cows forward, five turn and go backward. By the time we coax the five forward, the ones that were going ahead are on their way back. Now three of them are running sideways. Four forward. Two back again.

We yell. We plead. We cry. We swear. We promise the kingdom of heaven. But nothing we do, nothing we say keeps them moving straight ahead. They will not be ordered about, as if living in Hitler's barns has affected them, too.

There are dozens of cows, and each seems to have a mind of its own. The sun is shining. Our task is ridiculous. We haven't smiled for an eternity. Suddenly all hell breaks loose in us. We start to laugh hysterically. Chicha wields her stick and laughs. Rachel pursues a cow and laughs. I fall on the ground and laugh.

We laugh and joke. For all the world we are the happiest cattle herders in this rotten land. The cows do as they wish, while all that is pent up in us explodes in crazy, joyous laughter.

Finally, we calm down and make a determined effort to

regiment our charges. We succeed in driving the cattle a little farther ahead. Then the scene repeats itself. We gain an inch, we lose ten. We try again. We howl some more. The sun has set. It is getting late and cool. At last, we deliver the independent creatures to their destination.

With a job so well done, we return to our modest quarters and recount each scene amid new waves of laughter. We know now that we still can have fun, even if it takes a herd of cattle to make it happen. We are happy that we have relearned how to laugh.

vii

We will have to learn how to cry. . . .
But if we let the tears flow, how long would
we weep? For all eternity? For six million years?
The cows are gone. Now there is no basic food supply
from anywhere. The available food in the area keeps dimin-
ishing. Only the people absolutely necessary for managing
things will be permitted to remain. The others will have to
move on. They will have to try to make their way to their
various homelands.

We hope that the war will soon be won and trains will
become available. We have consumed everything edible.
Food that is scarce cannot be fairly divided. It is clear that
we will have to leave.

The Russians provide us with some kind of discharge

papers, attesting to our work record, or whatever. They seem regretful and honorable, but it doesn't satisfy us. We want to remain. Our minds understand that we must leave, but our emotions react in a deeply wounded way. In our hearts, we feel that the curse of the wandering Jew is upon us again.

viii

W e are desperate. We do not want to give up the relative security of what we have here. For six weeks we have had some kind of home. Diabolical, ironic that we should consider as something good an abandoned house in this vile land.

It is still cold and wintry. We know that no one is waiting for us at home in Hungary. If Cipi and Philip are alive, they know that, too. If ever we can go anywhere, we will go to America, to New York, to our father, our only living parent.

We love being liberated. We think of the Russian soldiers as life-givers. They kept the Germans from annihilating us. They are responsible for our reentering life. They let no dogs loose on us. They let no Dr. Mengele loose on us. Their smoke emits the smell of food, not the scent of burning flesh.

Now they are imploring us to leave. When we procrasti-
nate, they order us to go.

"We need more healing."

"Food is scarce. Can't you see that?"

"Yes, but we are afraid. Let us stay a little longer."

Our pleas are to no avail. We must leave, like all the
others. We will join the road people until we find a train
that will deliver us to a land of peace.

Where is that land of peace? How long are we to wander
before we can cry ourselves to sleep on our own pillows?

We organize and organize until we accumulate a heap of
clothes. What to sort out, what to take on this, our new
unknown journey? What will be warm enough to fend off
the cold, light enough to carry, strong enough to protect
us?

The last time we made such decisions, we found ourselves at journey's end in the cannibal kingdom of Auschwitz. Where will this journey lead?

We are glum, contemplative. Our last march, the death
march, is still burned into the soles of our feet. We look for
an image of solace and come to rest on the hope that while
on the road, we might bump into the missing members of
our family.

We find a small wagon on which to load our belongings.
We load items, remove them, put them back again. It is so
difficult to part with any of our newfound riches. Our
wagon, we know, must not be overburdened. We will have
to pull it wherever we go, and our trip may be long and
wearisome. We choose, discard, reacquire. We have a special fondness for a large robe. It is dark red with white
checks. It is too heavy, but we pile it on the wagon.

Slowly we make peace with the prospect of living a road
life. There will be, we pray, compensating factors. We say

good-bye to those who remain, knowing well that we will never share good or bad again, and join the multinational, multilingual remnants of the bloodbath.

Almost immediately we begin to make friends and share the tales of common horrors.

"Which camp were you in? How many were in your family? How many survived? Who are you looking for? Do you have any hope?"

We talk and walk. We walk and remember. We walk and hurt. We wipe away tears that haven't surfaced yet. Sometimes we hum tunes.

Each day, as dusk approaches, we look for deserted homes to sleep in, homes that lodged yesterday's travelers. This kind of life calls for intuition and ingenuity. We have to share, be compassionate, crowd together, grab, run before others get there. Some villages yield an abundance of empty homes, others only a scant few.

We are helpful and kind to one another. The food we have brought along keeps us well. We keep walking during daylight, settle before dark.

On the third night we find shelter in a room with two large mattresses on the floor. A middle-aged woman joins us to share our "beds." She keeps talking about her twin daughters who were separated from her by Dr. Mengele upon their arrival at Auschwitz. She insists that her daughters are alive. Her faith in their survival is like a religious fervor.

We are skeptical, but we haven't the heart to tell her otherwise. We know that Mengele's particular passion was to perform medical experiments on twins.

We prepare for bed. Rachel and I take one mattress, Chicha and the woman the other. Suddenly, a drunken soldier enters the room. He sizes up the situation and chooses a bedmate. "*Chornaya*," he mutters, selecting Chicha, my dark-haired sister. He quickly undresses and turns out the light.

In the dark the middle-aged woman switches places with Chicha.

In the morning the soldier realizes the deception. He smiles, dresses, and departs. On his way out he tosses a gold watch to his most recent conquest. The woman becomes part of our wandering family.

Finally, we lose her on the road, and much later we learn that she has actually, miraculously, found her twins alive in Budapest.

On our journey the woman never stopped talking about her children. She was certain the gods had decreed that somewhere another mother would give her body to a drunken soldier, as she had done, to save her daughters' virginity. We shall always remember her faith. We do not remember her name.

ix

Our troubles seem to be lessening. From here on, no attempts are made to violate our bodies. The farther away we get from the gruesome face of war, the less often do the soldiers around us bury themselves in alcohol.

Now we try to converse with the Russians. We speak no Russian at all, except for the few words that ruled our lives while we were cow-tending: *"Nyet rabota, nyet khleba"*— "No work, no bread." Those words, literally, were our daily bread. We had no right, we were told, to expect unearned food; everyone must work. The Russian words were enough to spur us on to earn our food.

Upon passing through the gates at Auschwitz, we were confronted with the Nazi slogan *"Arbeit macht frei"*— "Work makes one free." The German words offered no nourishment, no spur, only freedom to work.

Whoever passed through those gates was treated to more

"freedom" than any mind is capable of conjuring up. Remembrance of the vile Nazi slogan, the insidious invitation to labor, the sick mockery, forces my eyes shut even decades later. By comparison, the Russian slogan was a lilting song of praise to human dignity.

With body gestures we now address the Russians. We communicate the fact that we do not speak their language.

"All right, so you can't *speak* our language, but surely you can *understand* it?"

The Russian logic makes us laugh.

The barrier of language becomes an enemy amid the desire for friendship between the liberators and the liberated. How strange that war can be funny, too.

The kilometers shrink while they seem endless. Our energies are ebbing. Is there no resting place for human beings as weary as we are? With each step our wagon seems to be heavier and harder to pull. We agonize over each treasure we are forced to eliminate.

Were we always walking? Were we born walking? Where is the end of the road? We are tired of dragging the whole of our lives in this stinking country of destruction.

We are still in Germany. We cannot walk fast enough to forever leave it behind. We would like to dissolve the road, for this is Hitler's *Reich*, and walking on this road of dirt contaminates our tired feet. We want to leap over this contaminated ground, swim the Atlantic to the New World, and cleanse ourselves of the filthy hate of Hitler in that great big body of water.

Each day the rising sun finds us on the road. Nearly till sunset, we walk in search of an elusive train. The bonds we cement en route have a built-in component—loss. For a

long time now, only loss seems to mark love. We touch,
emotions engage, then disengage again. All the marchers
are bound for different countries, different lives, and all
have common memories of pain.

Our truest search is for love, reentanglement with those
we loved. Everything is altered. All the road walkers want
is to protect their own. But for most of them there is no one
to protect. They walk alone.

We are fortunate. There are three of us. There were
more. They are no more. Hope flickers and fades. Perhaps
there will never be more, only the three of us and our father, if he is still alive in that far-off world of America.

Our father is all alone. What are his dreams? Does he lull
himself to sleep with unrealities? By now he must know the
truth—that Dr. Mengele devastated his people, that all of
his family could not still be alive. How does he live? Does
God help him?

We have grown so far from our father. The cruelest time,
we spent apart. If ever we see him, how should we greet
him?

"Hello, Father. We are alive. They are not."

How long have we been marching? Our aching legs know
the answer—many days, perhaps a week. It is the month of
March now.

March 1945 has nothing in common with the Marches
we used to know. March used to be springtime; falling-
in-love time; old-fashioned, romantic, serenading time;
leisure-walk time, up and down Main Street, in Kisvarda,
Hungary.

It was a time when I really didn't have to take a little
mirror from my purse to fix my hair. My hair didn't need
fixing. I just pretended. I just wanted to see in the mirror's

reflection whether that tall, lanky, newest fancy of mine was following me. My tiny town held all the wonders of the world for me—life, death, love.

Our steady, wearying journey now affords me a steady stream of time for contemplation. And I keep remembering.

x

There are six young people in my home: my four sisters, my one brother, myself. Our ages range from thirteen to somewhat past twenty. If God made all of us in His image, God must be filled with love of life, sizzling excitement, and curiosity.

We girls try on my aunt's large bra with nothing to fill it. We squabble. We make up.

Boys flock to our house. "Is Philip home?"

Liars!

They have come to check whether the five pairs of developing young bosoms have grown firmer, the hips rounder, the curves more graceful. They have come to tease and pinch and touch.

We make believe the boys are really friends of our brother. We are liars, too. We want them to look. We want them to feel.

Later they come to our home as young men, lying less, reaching gently for an arm to caress, lips to kiss, hair to smooth; engaging in the virginal games of the sexually restricted forties. The boys are there all the time, winter and summer.

In the winter we huddle together in front of our tall tile heating unit, which we continually feed with wooden logs. The radio blasts ugly news and delicious music. We move close to each other and gaze at the fire. We seek comfort from that other fire raging in the atmosphere. That other fire makes us shiver. That other fire has an icy name called Hitler.

We try to muffle Hitler's crackling with singing. We are forever singing the popular songs of the day.

Sandor drums away with his fingers and knuckles. He is a natural percussionist, using any chair in range as his musical instrument. He sings. He dances. From moment to moment he seizes one of us five girls and tangos around the kitchen table.

Lacy plays cards. Miki tells jokes. Harry philosophizes.

Cipi rouges her cheeks. Rachel braids her hair. Potyo licks honey from the honey jar.

Chicha writes poetry. Philip teaches Hebrew to his friends in the attic. I adjust my skirt and respond to a call for another dance.

My mother waits for a letter from America, from my father, and worries about Hitler.

We argue about politics, fight for first place in my mother's heart, and call her a pessimist. We put on snowshoes and, in groups of five, six, or seven, go out for romantic midnight strolls in the snow-covered, frozen world of Kisvarda.

Afterward we play dominoes, dance another dance, sing another song, and say good night. We stay up very late, extending time, for our lives may be short.

In the summer we no longer go to the Carpathian Mountains, so we tan ourselves bronze in our war-clouded backyard. We pour buckets of water on each other from the ever-full barrel of rainwater outside our house. We spend much time frolicking at home—our courtyard has had to replace our Carpathian vacation land.

Kazi lives at the other end of our yard. He and I are in love. His balcony is higher than mine. He can look down on me. I can look up to him. We have looked at each other for years, but we have never actually met. We would have had to meet formally, and we couldn't. We come from totally different worlds.

Hungary is a fiercely anti-Semitic country. I am a middle-class Jewish girl, Kazi an aristocratic Gentile. If friendship between two such different people can exist, it has to be in a large city where people can submerge their identities without notice. Kisvarda is a very small town, too small for things so large, so complex. So I just love Kazi from afar.

I spend endless hours on my balcony, looking up at his balcony while he looks down at me. Kazi is tall, blond, lean, strong. Kazi is beautiful.

We love and never meet. We love and never talk. We love and never touch.

What happened to you, Kazi? Could you, too, have been an anti-Semite? And, if so, why did I love you, Kazi?

Chicha, did I, too, love your boyfriend Gyuszi? I don't remember. I only remember the pain I felt when I saw you cry, when news of his death came. You couldn't stop crying.

The Germans had used him as a human "mine detector" on the Russian front. They forced him, as well as other Jewish slaves, to walk across open fields in advance of German tanks. When he stepped on a hidden mine, his small body and large eyes were blown into smithereens.

Was there a face more beautiful and a pen more poetic? You held on to his poems as though adoring a god. And you wrote poetry to him when there was no Gyuszi anymore. Chicha, did you ever again love anyone the way you loved him?

I must stop remembering. I must keep walking into the future, with blisters forming on my feet, in this ugly foreign land.

I must stop remembering. . . .

xi

Our blisters hurt. However urgent the future, we must rest for a day. We say good-bye to our week-old friends of the road. We will join the next group of future-pursuers on the morrow.

Immediately, I forget my determination not to remember, and I think of my mother. I hear her voice again: "Hitler will lose the war, children, but he will win it against the Jews."

I remember my mother's extraordinary social consciousness, her involvement with the fate of mankind. My mother could barely squeeze her vision into the narrow confines of our age. Her mind was bursting with the largeness of the future. The twentieth century was too narrow and too cruel for her.

We were the young people in our home, but my mother was the embodiment of what the spirit of youth should be.

Her physical needs were modest, but her expectations from the human species were immodest and visionary. What haunted her was the fear that human beings might fail to measure up to their potential.

On that ugly ride in the cattle car that delivered her into Mengele's inferno, she had an unforgettable look of hope and prayer for her children, combined with total resignation about the days left for her. She didn't know about Auschwitz, as none of us knew, but she knew that something horrendous would be the culmination of that insane journey.

How could she have known about Auschwitz? In our anti-Semitic, Nazi-sympathizing country, there was no negative publicity about Hitler and his deeds. The German *Führer* ranted of glory, not of Auschwitz, over Hungary's airwaves.

Filthy Jews! Heil Hitler! Jews! Jews! Heil Hitler!

Those were the deafening sounds thundering out of Hungary's radio. The fascist lies that were spewed forth spoke of Hitler, the *Ubermensch*, not of German crematoriums. The Jews had no special envoys whispering the real truth in their ears. Jews knew only what Hitler and his henchmen wanted them to know.

And had we known what was happening, what could we possibly have done? The world was not clamoring or rallying to save us. We were utterly alone, unorganized, and unarmed—children, women, the old, the sick; our able-bodied men had been taken away from us as slave laborers years ago. When the trained armies of every European country had fallen before the German beasts, could we weak civilian remnants have fought the Nazis with our shoelaces, our spoons, our pencils?

I squint my eyes in agony as the road seems to narrow in the distance. In the past few weeks thousands have walked this way. Their life-affirming steps echo a legacy of encouragement to those who follow. But my pain and anger keep intruding, however hard I try to fix my gaze on the road that is supposed to deliver me into the future.

History is tugging at my head. It invades the entire inner territory of my mind. If freedom is inner, then I am not free. I never will be. We are walking in a country that violated everything free men ever stood for, violated even our ability to enjoy freedom, for it imprisoned our memories in a permanent hideous way. I am sure that we will try to break free, but the images in our heads are so powerful, they probably will not respond to the healing of time; they probably will be our companions until we die.

Our flesh seems to have responded better. Almost immediately after our escape, we began to put on weight. We forced insane amounts of food into our hardly used stomachs. We abused our bellies pitifully; nonetheless, we grew stronger, fatter, and healthier with each mouthful. Whatever ailed us, we medicated with food. The food made us both ill and well.

It is so wonderful to see the contours and adornments of our bodies again—bosoms, head hair, underarm hair, pubic hair. The human beings on the road no longer look like *Musulmans*, like walking skeletons. That is all we were used to seeing, except for the attack dogs and the Nazi dogs. We seem to have been on a journey to a bizarre planet, and now we are back again. Will we be allowed to conclude our insane journey and be able to die in bed? An image of children surrounding the bedside of a dying

41

parent is so comforting. Will we ever reach that stage of comfort?

The roads are alive with seemingly large numbers of people, but in comparison to those who were murdered, they are but a handful. The marchers are not only the survivors of the death camps, but others, too—partisans, freed political prisoners, Jews who had been hiding for years with false identity papers, liberated allied soldiers from around the globe, and, probably, some Nazis in disguise, mingling in our midst as victims, seeking to escape retribution.

We are unable to weed the Nazis out and wonder whether any authority anywhere will ever be able to cut through their false papers, their fairy tales, their lies. Some, no doubt, will be unmasked; most, probably, will not. Will they sit next to me on a bus in a far-off land someday? In America? Will they live on the same street where I am nurturing my children? Will Dr. Mengele breathe the same air as my family? The thought is shattering. Will the Nazis, with altered features, live happily and commingle with us in a grocery store, in a theater?

We wore yellow stars to single us out.

What will they wear?

xii

We are still in Germany, marching toward a magic train that will take us away from here. German pebbles hurt our feet, and everything else. We vow never to set foot here again. With each step, we are nearer the blessed train, but not near enough to feel peaceful. Peace might come, perhaps, when we inhale the smoke of the locomotive. Wearily we trudge on, till the end of day, to start anew in the morning.

Almost two weeks have passed since we left Jagadschutz on foot. The war has not yet ended, but we are certain now that it will. In a sense it has ended for us. We are beyond the reach of the Nazis. Their struggle with the Russians and the Allies is far enough to the rear for us not to worry. The Germans are not about to return.

We are now at the outskirts of a town whose name, we learn, is Oelsk, or something that sounds like Oelsk. No town has a greater lure, for, incredibly, there are railroad tracks leading into it.

Soon a train is within view.

A vision of that other train, a train of crowded cattle cars and death, appears in my head. I force the image from my mind and conjure up another vision, a childhood memory of a choo-choo train bearing my mother, my grandmother, and the six of us children to the Carpathian Mountains for a summer vacation. Did we really have a childhood, or were we always prisoners? I try to ease the pain of the present, but it doesn't really work. We are where we are. We are where we have been, lugging a few rags we can discard and a mammoth monster we cannot—Auschwitz. It was there that we were sewn together emotionally. It is that oneness, forged in fire, love tended to in such a place of hate that perhaps led us to escape from the death march and on to this life march.

I look at my sisters and remember their acts of goodness, their fear and bravery. I remember how Rachel donned an armor of fearlessness right after liberation to conceal her terror. She stuck a knife in one boot and announced, "No one will ever harm me again!"

She has not parted with the knife, nor has she had to use it. Could she if she had to?

We draw strength from this young avenger. I look at her with loving prayers. May no harm come to this child, God. She has suffered so much. She must have some laughter still tucked away in her. Her sense of humor used to keep us sane throughout the difficult years. She stopped laughing in Auschwitz.

I look at Chicha in awe. She is indomitable, the most faithful replica of my mother, reflecting my mother's resolute vision of a better age. Is Chicha's faith justified? Can a faith so abused save itself? I look at her pleadingly for an answer. Help me restore my faith, Chicha. Why is your faith not more shaken? Where do you get it?

You are so small of frame, Chicha. You are so big, damn it! How could you have shared the way you did in Auschwitz, where there was nothing to share, save suffering? How could you have said, "I really am not hungry," and given me a morsel of your morsel? I couldn't have done it. You, like me, weighed no more than forty or fifty pounds. Yet you were able to say, "I am not hungry."

Will mothers like ours and daughters like you save the soul of humankind? What would the world, littered with inhumanity, be without a few like you? We need those like you to help us heal the Earth.

Perhaps it is worth living, after all.

xiii

I must think of goodness, else I cannot go on. I reach for my friend Manyi in my mind.

Manyi was working in the *Unterkumpft* at the time we arrived at Auschwitz. The *Unterkumpft* was the temporary hoarding place, the warehouse, for all the fine things we brought along from our homes and which were confiscated by the Nazis upon our arrival.

The stolen possessions and clothing had to be sorted in the warehouse before shipment to the good people of that good Germany. The *Unterkumpft* was an isolated building with pleasant living quarters for the Nazi in charge. For his personal comfort the Nazi needed a maid, a cook, and whatever else—and Manyi was that maid and cook and whatever else.

Manyi was kept well fed, not like us. She looked like an actual woman. She was beautiful and good. That "whatever else" enabled her not only to live, but also to get me and several other girls jobs sorting clothes. Those jobs had very small, but very important, benefits.

Each time we entered or left the *Unterkumpft*, we were frisked. At times, however, at great risk, it was possible to sneak out a knife or other small item in our shoes to barter for a crumb of bread from a miserable creature out in the camp. A prisoner with a knife had the possibility of self-deception. She could slice her wretched portion of "daily bread," a mixture of flour and sawdust, into paper-thin slices, thus making it appear to be more than it really was and enabling the slices to be apportioned for the day.

The apportionment, however, like the slicing, didn't work. It was impossible to maintain the self-deception for long. We were too hungry.

"I will save this slice for the afternoon, that one for the evening."

Such promises could not be kept. The torture of eyeing the slices, touching them, and pulling the hands back again was intolerable. We touched a slice and stole the corner. We touched again and stole again. Thus, we kept stealing our own hard-earned bread.

When I got desperately ill with typhus and couldn't re-port to work, Manyi sneaked Chicha into the *Unterkumpft* in my stead. Such a breach of the "holy" Nazi rules could have cost Manyi her life, or, at the least, her "whatever else" job. The job was important to her, both for her own sake and for what it enabled her to do to help her fellow prisoners. Not that she had a choice about her fate; she had none—she was chosen to kiss the depraved, and relatively few were chosen for this dubious honor.

Is a lice-filled bag of bones a woman, an object of desire? With the exception of a few—people working in the kitchens, kapos, the handful of women singled out for German lust—we all were just such bags of bones. Can anyone imagine a lice-filled walking skeleton as a goddess of love?

Manyi, good Manyi, you should have lived. Your beastly Nazi lover, your lover of hate, should have died.

I am free now. Why do I keep harking back to that terrible terrain again and again? Are those memories forever encased within me and I shall never be free?

Someone, please, tear my inner dungeon and let me out. I want to be free. It is close to springtime. Let me smell the flowers, inhale the perfume of earth's creations, not Dr. Mengele's stench.

I want to be free, Doctor. You controlled me in your gruesome prison. Don't control my freedom. I want you dead not only in reality, but in memory, too. I want you excised from all of us. When will that be? In which millennium? Once and for all, will I ever be able to say, "Goodbye, Dr. Mengele?"

I won't last out this century. Will our children be able to forget what we shall tell them? Will we have the heart to tell them what we know? We will have to, because history cannot be trusted. It distorts. Will anyone believe the unbelievable?

We are within inches of the train in Oelsk as my mind pokes and probes. We can touch the train. It is not made up of cattle cars. It is a crazy, wonderful train with regular cars, with bunklike arrangements for sleeping, with a huge cauldron of food being mixed by a rosy-cheeked woman soldier of the Russian Army. She has the kindly, smiling face of a heavy mama. Nourish us, dear mama. We are still very hungry.

Will our hunger ever subside enough to enable us to

order a normal meal in a restaurant? Will we ever use a fork and knife, or will we always gobble? Will I ever be able to mix food with conversation, put down my fork long enough to finish a sentence? Do people talk at mealtime, or do they eat, eat, eat?

Hail to food. I have no time to talk.

Part Two

En Route to Odessa

xiv

We begin to climb aboard the train, we and the others, the dear others from around the globe: Jews who weren't murdered, and liberated soldier prisoners, soldiers who killed in order to stop Hitler from murdering us. Tall Englishman, short Hindu, blond Scot, smiling American, Palestinian Jew, Sino-European, Czech Jewess, French fighter, people from tiny hamlets and great nations—and three Jewish girls from Kisvarda, Hungary. All these, plus the Russian soldiers responsible for our journey and our liberation.

Our commonality is overwhelming. We are all survivors of the same disease, hate. In this moving venture we nourish each other with care and concern. There is no common language between us, yet we speak the same tongue. With the touch of a hand, a comforting gesture, a look, we understand each other's recent past.

Those who are returning to their homes and families seem fully to comprehend that we three—Rachel, Chicha, and I—and the other liberated Jewish survivors are a breed separate and apart. No one will be brewing coffee, serving drinks, baking bread and cookies for us at the end of our journey, wherever that end will be. Families will not be waiting for us; no one will be sitting around listening to our war stories. Our mothers and fathers did not accumulate letters from us while we were gone. There will be no parties to celebrate our kind of heroism. There will be no music and no neighbors weeping with joy for us, no salty tears for our dead.

Wherever we go, we will be alien orphans. Home is nowhere for us—not in our native land, not in any new land that will have us. We will have to learn a new language, a new culture, a new mode of dress and behavior. We will have to learn to control the rage inside us or make peace with it. We will have to learn how to communicate the unbelievable or keep silent and make believe that we just happened upon this side of the ocean or the other.

In this train we have an identity: we are little girls from a big war. On the other side of the ocean, should we ever reach that haven, we will be the strangest of strangers, from a continent of killing that contained within it yet other continents called Auschwitz and Bergen-Belsen and other strange names.

The Hindu sits in the lotus position and never talks. Does he ever sleep? It doesn't seem so. The Czech Jewess falls in love with the tall Englishman. The Palestinian promises the blessings of the kibbutz, the whole kibbutz, to Rachel. The New Zealander promises New Zealand to Chicha. And Les, the dearest, gentlest American soldier, mothers me with the most exquisite sensitivity.

Les is about twenty-two, a little older than I, but he adopts me as though I were an infant in need of ceaseless care. He must have seen Auschwitz or some other death camp, for he looks at me in total awe. In his every move he seems determined to somehow make up for the ferocious crime committed against me.

For two weeks, as the train rolls toward Odessa, Les seems to suspend his own person so that all he has, all he is, can be put in the service of healing. I don't think he is in love with me—he *is* love, total love. He provides something warm for my shoulders, something cool to quench my thirst, something nourishing to make me gain weight. Where does he get it all?

Each time the train stops, Les disappears and comes back with the sweetest balms. His delicacy is so unique that everyone is touched by it. Never have I seen such gentleness, as if some mysterious force willed the antithesis of Auschwitz upon me. Les asks for nothing in exchange.

I wonder now, so many years later, how much that young American was able to glean from my awe of him, from the depth of my loving appreciation, from my loving gratitude.

For two weeks the train keeps stopping in all kinds of places for all kinds of intervals. We visit with the other riders; by now, we all feel like kin. We do not understand the logistics of travel in a war-torn land. Are the frequent stops necessary for the movement of more urgent cargo in the other direction? Ammunition? Guns? The war is still in progress. It is March 1945. When will the war end? Are there concentration camps still to be liberated? Is Cipi in one of them? Is Philip?

War is noisy as hell, but it is silent concerning its secrets.

It is so hard to find out anything. Gossip of great victories abounds. We love the stories. Are they true? Will the war be over soon?

The train is very long. Masses of people are riding on it, but we have all been on board for so long that to us it is a traveling community. Food is available or not. The motherly Russian cook concocts a magic all-in-one meal whenever she gets a delivery of ingredients from who-knows-where. In her huge cauldron she stirs vegetables and meat with a giant wooden spoon. We watch her prepare the "family meal" with delicious excitement. If only food were cooking around the clock . . . but it is not.

On some days we are terribly hungry. We talk about nothing but food. We are frustrated by the British. They alone seem to be different. They do not complain. They talk about the weather, the dog that runs past the train, the countryside—anything but food. Were they not to eat for a year, it seems, they would not complain. They are stony-faced at the mention of food. What makes them the way they are? Why can't they say they are hungry?

In certain villages the train stops long enough for us to go to the open farmers' markets, which are filled with the aroma of the morning's harvest. The peasants are kindly, but we have no money. We hardly remember what money looks like.

The peasants have food but lack clothing. We barter our stockings and other items from the "wardrobe" we dragged along from the blacksmith's house. Some peasants want our stockings more than anything else. We do not understand why. We barter with them for eggs and return to our train home.

In a battered pan, Rachel collects scalding water droplets from the steam plumes of the locomotive. We keep the eggs in the hot water long enough to half cook them, then enjoy a sumptuous feast; we are happy again.

We roll along and stop again. We barter for potatoes and cook them in an instant fireplace of burning twigs. They are tastier, it seems, than any dish that any gourmet chef could prepare. Our battered pan is lovable and lickable whenever sticky food graces its contours.

We are happy with our lot, with our train, with our companions. The Russian cook is cooking again. We love her food. We love her.

At each stop, romance is refueled. We roll cigarettes and stroll flirtatiously in the sun. Our hair has grown a bit. We can actually begin to use a comb. We have not had any use for one in nearly a year. It is an uncanny sensation.

We stroll beside the train displaying our short crowns of an inch of hair. With our newly found womanhood, we attract the attention of the men of our world. We are our very attractive selves again, and the soldiers on our train admire us, are ready to whisk us away to cities and hamlets we have never heard of.

But our plans are different. We have yet to search, to find parts of our old family before we try to create a new one. Our yearnings are fixed on what was: Cipi, Philip, my father.

Innocent, global flirtations en route to Odessa are such fun, but we are on our way to America, not Australia, New Zealand, or India. We are looking for Kisvarda. We will go all the way to America to try to find it. We are not in love yet, only intrigued by the very real possibility that someday we will be.

As I sit on the train, Les sensitively bandages my inner wounds. Chicha and Rachel report on new conquests. "I was proposed to," says Chicha. "So was I," says Rachel.

All a beautiful thing has to do is get off the train for a walk and she gets a marriage proposal. However playful and unserious these promises of heaven are, they nurture the long-dead womanhood in us, and we are grateful to these Don Juans of a devastating war. May you never war again, handsome soldiers. May this train, with its gathering of exiles, travel into an age of peace. We are all so tired.

XV

The train pulls into a large railroad station. It is Lemberg. A moment of affection for Lemberg: it is the city of an old family friend.

The early spring day turns cool. People around the station pull their clothing closer to their bodies. Everything—the station, the weather, the people—looks gray.

An enormous number of gapers are idling about. They seem jobless, purposeless, tired of the war. They, like us, are liberated. Why does the air around them feel so heavy, so overwhelmed with defeat?

As we have done at many stops, we get off the train for our exploratory stroll, eager for life-affirming scenes, sounds, gestures, words. Suddenly, we are assaulted by a repressed, staccato hiss: *Jews! Jews! Jews!* Sullen townspeople in our path are spewing their hatred at us.

Whoever wants to stroll, don't stroll in Lemberg. Don't

stroll where the residue of hate mars the night in March. Don't stroll where people know not when to stop. Don't stroll in "never-enough" places.

Is there any place to stroll?

We are frightened and run back to the love we have come to know on the train. As the train pulls out, we cry thick unwipeable tears. The liberated soldiers with us, who fought against just this kind of hatred, are angry enough to want to shoot again. We want to run to the outer perimeters of this world and leap over to another.

The train is too slow. We want to reach a safer town. Is there one? Everyone around us is sad and frustrated. They comfort us with compassion mixed with anger. They do what they can to ease our pain, realizing that the good battle is not yet over. Perhaps it never will be.

Rachel, Chicha, and I draw close to each other. We remember too much at the very time we desperately want to learn the art of forgetting. Full of sadness, we drop off to sleep. When we awake, we are reassured by the gentle smiles of our guardians. We are out of Lemberg.

When next we stop, our steps are less nimble as we alight from the train. We inch our way with caution and are happy to sense neither love nor hate. We try to force Lemberg out of our fragile, wounded hearts. At each subsequent stop, we gain more confidence. We recover our spirit, begin to smile, and show off our aliveness. Look, everybody: we didn't let them kill us.

The train huffs and puffs to its destination. Each time it whistles, it heralds the arrival of the live ones, the ones who dared to outlive Hitler.

A meager lunch is served in a cheerful place in the next town. There are napkins on the table. To us the service seems almost elegant. Still, we gobble down our food while the English fuss with the proprieties of "dining." Leisurely and time-consumingly, they ceremoniously lift their forks with the left hand, cut tiny portions with the right hand, and chew minuscule bites. We don't understand.

At another stop, we see a hefty Russian woman operating a crane. The sight of the woman in such a masculine job is new to us. We marvel at her efficiency and are amused by this unfamiliar reversal of roles. Suddenly, the woman cups her hands in front of her mouth and yells, "Do you have silk stockings? I'll give you rubles in exchange."

We find a pair, and the woman's smudged face lights up. We complete the transaction and joyfully speculate about the food we will purchase at the next marketplace.

The Russian woman puts her arm into the stockings, looking for imperfections, then lovingly folds and tucks them into her bosom. Feeling like capitalists, we count and fondle our rubles. Then, because we have neither purses nor pockets, we, too, tuck our treasure into our bosoms.

Such a colorful, bartering journey is not likely to be repeated on trips we shall take in our civilized life to come. But right now we are truly enjoying this upside-down joyride as a funny, twisted gift of war.

Our spirits are healthy on the train for a variety of reasons, but the prime one has to be that this dearest of trains is delivering us out of a land of shame. In Germany we couldn't clear our lungs. The oxygen we inhaled there felt like a disease. Living needs fresh air. Germany emitted an air of death.

For our new life we must cross the ocean. We must put the cleansing waters of the sea between us and where we have been. It is true that disease can spread from country to country, but perhaps it cannot cross the ocean. I conjure a vision of great white waves blocking my view of Germany. I hear the roaring sea drowning out the roars of evil memory: *Heil, Hitler! Heil, Hitler!*

Now the train, with its sounds of deliverance, comes to rest in a big Russian city, and we are invited for a big treat. We are lined up for a long walk through bombed-out neighborhoods. It is a city sizzling with life. Clearing of rubble is going on everywhere to the blaring sounds of news and music emanating from a public address system. The thunder of rousing military marches invigorates our steps as we arrive at a huge farm.

The Russians guide us through the technological wonders of a "modern" farm. We detect their pride, even as we do not comprehend their language. Most of us are not interested in their latest agricultural machinery, but we feel like dancing at the sight of the generous farm-fresh spread they have prepared for us.

Thank you, Russians. Thank you for liberating us. Thank you for the food. Good luck with your harvest. There is friendship and laughter. With our stomachs deliciously full, we practically dance our way back to our train.

xvi

We don't know what Odessa will bring. Our emotions are scrambled. We know that our newfound friends will soon scatter, and the gentleness and love we were nourished on during these past two weeks will seep out of our lives. The cuddling comfort we felt will dissipate in the reality of separation.

We spend the last few hours of our long train odyssey jotting down names and addresses. We have no location to give, unless our father is still alive at 166 Ross Street. We make promises of lifelong loyalty, of remembering, knowing full well that distances and time tend to erode promises.

Still, it is good to know that in a far-off corner of the world, somebody, for a while, will remember the color of our eyes, the tears we shed, the smiles we smiled, and our determination to live. It is good to know that our names will be remembered, because for so long we were just concentration camp numbers: 79212, 79213, 79214.

The number 79215 belongs to Cipi. Cipi, where are you? We busy ourselves with our belongings. We have bartered away so much that our worldly treasures are light to carry. We help each other. We no longer sell or buy. We give gifts. We give affection.

The train screeches to a halt. Odessa.

We don't know how we will be transported from the railroad station, or where. Inevitably, there will be some chaos with so many people alighting simultaneously from our home in motion.

We quickly hug our friends and anyone else in our farewell path of affection. Chicha, Rachel, and I lock hands for fear that in the commotion we might be separated.

'Bye . . . when peace will come, we'll drink to you.

Noisy arrangements, preparations of all kinds are in progress for our transportation to a rehabilitation center. It is late afternoon, very chilly, April 4, 1945.

The Germans said, "*Mach schnell.*" The Russians keep saying, "*Davai, davai,*" or something like it. It seems to mean, "Move quickly." A half-track pulls up. We climb in and are off. The famous Black Sea city of Odessa is bleak, gray, and in rubble. The route we take is in rubble.

The last time we were in a half-track was when we were hauled to Birnbaumel by the Nazis in November 1944. This half-track triggers my memory. We are back in a clearing in a German forest. A host of shivering bones are swaying fragilely in the wintry air. One thousand pitiful creatures, straight from Auschwitz.

Ominous sky. Gray, frozen patch of earth in Nazidom's

kingdom. Fat, armed SS men in earnest, momentous conferences. A pile of shovels on the ground.

Yes, we know what all this means. The shovels are to dig our own graves, pits for our bullet-ridden bodies. Did the beasts have to drag us this far for manual killing when the gas chambers and crematoriums were so close at hand at Auschwitz? Or was the murder machinery made inoperative just before we left that dread hell of extermination, or right afterward?

The Germans are the masters of cunning, forever altering their diabolical plans so that we should not be able to outsmart them. As if we could. We were never smart, evil, or devious enough to figure them out. They were smarter and certainly more evil—as when they enticed prisoners, with promises of bread, to voluntarily go on transport. And the following day, the duped prisoners' clothing would come back from the crematoriums.

We weren't murdered in Birnbaumel, but most of the thousand bags of bones perished finally on the snowy death march to Bergen-Belsen.

We promised our friends on the train to try not to remember. Promises are easily broken.

We are on half-tracks again; but now we are garbed in warm clothing, we are not hungry, and our liberators are trying to take care of us. Our lives are not being threatened.

We are in a great city. Why is my memory so stubborn?

We pass the world-renowned opera house. We see a sad-looking city trying to repair its buildings, trying to regain its soul. We see bundled-up children and adults silently welcoming us, the gaping strangers, as we roll by them.

We have been en route for an eternity. We came by foot, by rail, via half-track. Hitler sent us. Thank you for your welcome.

We arrive at the rehabilitation center. The building is enormous, housing an enormous number of displaced people. We are led to a huge room that is filled with sleeping arrangements all over the floor. Languages abound. There are people, people everywhere. There are noises, excitement, expectations. There are new encounters, new friends, new hopes. The same questions.

"Where do you come from?"

"How long were you in Auschwitz?"

"When were you liberated? Where?"

"How many were in your family?"

"How many survived?"

"Where are you going?"

The variety of tales is staggering, as is the number of nationalities present. Not all the people are Jews. Not all are liberated soldiers. Not all are liberated slave laborers.

They are people from everywhere, human beings left over from Hitler's devastating rampage across the continents. The atmosphere is exciting, confusing, and life-affirming, with death and tragedy lurking everywhere in the background.

Chicha has a fever. A Russian doctor attends to her right away.

"Don't be frightened. It's just a bad cold," he comforts in Yiddish. "She'll be well soon. Where are you from?"

"Hungary. We were in Auschwitz. We're Jews."

"I'm a Jew, too. I live here in Odessa. Are you going back to Hungary?"

"Never. We want to go to America."

"I have a brother in America. Will you take a letter to him?"

The doctor is overworked. The Jewish survivors flock to

him. They have heard he is Jewish. They are eager to seek solace from a real doctor, a Jewish doctor, one who heals— not a killing doctor, like Dr. Mengele, the Nazi vulture of death.

We tell the Russian healer about Dr. Mengele. He already knows about him. He is in pain.

"Are you sure he is a physician?"

"Yes, we are absolutely certain. Mengele is a physician."

We try to go outside the center. The place is guarded. We are allowed to stand in front of the building for only a few minutes.

I wonder how many Nazis are in the building posing as survivors. I force the thought out of my mind. It is too painful. I cannot deal with it. It is too diabolical. I must stop thinking of anything but America.

xvii

It is still April 4, 1945. We spend the rest of the day and
night searching, querying. We want answers to all our
questions. We want to meet everyone, to find out about
life, about death, to discover who has plans for the future,
who hasn't. Almost everyone wants to go home.

Don't the death-camp survivors know that there is no one
at home?

They refuse to accept the fact. It is worth going home on
the slimmest chance that someone, someone, just might be
alive. Without hope it is not worth being anywhere.

In our wanderings through the rehab center, we meet a
liberated prisoner of war—slight, short, Yiddish-speaking
—a uniformed officer from the Royal Air Force. We tell
him who we are, where we come from, that our father is in
America. We tell him that, unlike all the others who want
to go home, we want to go to America. We tell him that if

Cipi and Philip, our oldest sister and only brother, are alive anywhere, we are absolutely certain that they, too, will want to go to America. But we don't know what to do about it. The official routine seems to be to send the refugees back to their countries of origin.

The British officer understands everything. He leaves us and returns with instructions: "Meet me here tomorrow morning at nine A.M. We have an appointment with the American military attaché. I will be your translator. I will help you in every way I can."

The attaché is handsome, intelligent, in control. Each of his questions is translated into Yiddish by the British flier, who is as concerned, as loyal, as if he were a lifelong friend. Having grown up as a Jew in fascist Hungary, I cannot remember a time when we were not afraid of an official. Now these two kind men are able to peel away that ingrained fear. We don't understand how men in uniform, so highly placed, can be so human.

Our whole horrendous experience unfolds in our answers to the questions, which keep coming at us. Each answer saddens the faces of the two men. The interview is long, and the longer it lasts, the closer the five of us feel to one another. We feel comfortable with our new British and American friends. We feel their compassion. We are all very civilized and very sad.

"There will be a ship leaving for America in sixteen days," the American attaché finally says. "You will be on that ship."

Our appointment is over.

Beaming, our British friend guides us back to our quarters. I don't remember seeing him again. I don't remember his name. I will never forget him.

Rachel, Chicha, and I hug each other with love and laughter. We are crazily happy. Incredulous. We are going to America. Can such good fortune happen to us with so much grace and speed?

We become instant celebrities—"the three Americans." We have status, happiness, and security. Three homeless, wandering, persecuted Jews have been invited to the New World!

We didn't have to beg. We were accepted. The good man said we would be on that ship. We run through the corridors of the refugee center, kissing Europeans.

"Did you hear? We are Americans! We are Americans!"

Sixteen days. Is that time enough for us to begin to believe there is a country that really wants us to live on its soil? Can we come to terms in such a short period with happiness, unused to joy as we are? Is it time enough for us to say good-bye to a continent that shaped and ruined our lives?

Everything within us is dancing to a lilting song: *You are not despised. You are accepted. You are welcome.*

The song we sing in return is: *Thank you, America. Thank you.*

We sing our way back to our communal bedroom. We are joyfully exhausted. Chicha is still feverish. We lie down to daydream, to relive each moment of this momentous day.

Suddenly, there is a knock on the door. It is the American military attaché, accompanied by two American soldiers carrying three army duffel bags.

"You are leaving for the United States on the S. S. *Brand Whitlock* tomorrow at eight A.M.," the attaché informs us.

71

"We've run out of female uniforms, but I've brought along our smallest-size male uniforms. I hope they fit you."

Three army uniforms, caps and all, appear from the duffel bags.

"I'm really sorry," the attaché continues, "but Liberty ships cannot have civilians aboard, so you'll have to dress like WACs. I'll be here in the morning to take you to the pier."

Just as suddenly as he appeared, the attaché departs, leaving the two soldiers behind to help us pack our belongings.

We are in total shock, verging on hysteria. But the shock does not last long. We begin to examine our "wardrobe," acting like American millionaires. We sort our treasures and give gifts to some of the girls we are leaving behind. In the face of our great good fortune, our restraint is minimal.

Our joyful mood lasts half the night. Parting from the others in the morning will be less painful than it was aboard the train, when our future was so fragile. We are now more self-assured, less tearful, less vulnerable. For the first time in our short lives, we go to sleep feeling like Americans.

Part Three

Crossing the Ocean

xviii

O dessa, April 6, 1945, 8:00 A.M. Dressed in khaki, we are on our way to the pier in an American jeep driven by the American military attaché. On the road I try to piece together the course of events that led up to this moment. I am unable to do so; things have moved so swiftly in the last forty-eight hours. Later, however, I learn what may have happened.

Apparently the American military attaché was so moved by our story that he contacted his superiors in Washington to ascertain whether our father was indeed living in the United States. Our story proved to be accurate, and the attaché was instructed to place us aboard the first vessel bound for America.

The S.S. *Brand Whitlock*, which had unloaded a cargo of tanks for the Russians, was leaving the next morning, and the attaché quickly arranged for our passage, together with sixteen liberated American soldiers and a German-American woman who was returning to the States from her fatherland. The woman had been a Nazi sympathizer, although a naturalized U. S. citizen. When Hitler was riding high, she had gone back to Germany to partake in the glory, but now that her erstwhile hero was losing the war, she was scurrying back to her American haven.

At dockside Rachel, Chicha, and I, trim in our new military uniforms, alight from the jeep. It can probably not be disputed that we look very attractive. While the attaché boards the ship for last-minute arrangements, the American crewmen on deck, beholding us below, can barely control their delight.

Each face welcomes us. Each wears a smile. We, once despised Jewish girls, are suddenly a delicious sight. We are not abused, lice-filled vermin. Life seems unreal.

It must be real, however, for we feel both the joy of *now* in every vein, and the pain of *then*. Bless you, dear strangers, as you gaze down upon us with affection and curiosity, as we stand in awesome anticipation, as we look up with hope.

The attaché returns and accompanies us to our new home, a floating heavenly home, that will sail on and on and on . . . to America. The attaché introduces us to the various officers and to the captain, who escorts us to a cabin that has been arranged for us.

"Have a pleasant trip," we hear the attaché saying as he shakes hands with us. Then we see him running down the gangplank.

I want to run after him, to hug and kiss him. I want to send a message with him to Hitler, wherever he sits on his disintegrating throne of disaster: "Sir, just one more thing, please. Please tell Adolf that my sisters and I are on the

S.S. *Brand Whitlock*, sailing to America. And, dear sir, we thank you. We thank you ever so much."

I don't move, however, and I never see that good American man again.

Dr. Mengele, we are on our way to America, and we are going to forget every brutal German word you forced us to learn. We are going to learn a new language. We are going to ask for bread and milk in Shakespeare's tongue. We will learn how to live speaking English and forget how people die speaking German.

The ship detaches itself from land and plunges into the waves of the Black Sea. "Good-bye, Dr. Mengele, you murderer. You robbed us of our family. Seven of us were supposed to go to America. Only three of us are leaving."

I search the sky to see if I can conjure up my mother and my little sister, Potyo. I look in desperate sorrow but can discern no human form. The smoke has vanished. There is not a trace. No grave. Nothing. Absolutely nothing.

My mother lived for just a while—Potyo for less than fourteen years. In a way they didn't really die. They simply became smoke.

How does one bury smoke?

How does one place headstones in the sky?

How does one bring flowers to the clouds?

Mother, Potyo . . . I am trying to say good-bye to you. I am trying to say good-bye.

Will Cipi and Philip ever sail the seas?

The captain seats the German-American woman and me at his table, Rachel at the next table. Jack, an officer and the only Jew aboard, instructs the steward to seat Chicha at his table. Later, when we get to know him better, Jack tells us why.

"While you were standing on the pier," he tells us, "I sized you up from the deck.

"This one's cute," he says, pointing to Rachel.

"That one's beautiful," he continues.

"But she's the one for me," he concludes, smiling at Chicha.

The captain, sensing my discomfort because of the German woman's presence, is solicitous and kind. He anticipates my needs and pays special attention to me. Still, for reasons I do not understand, I discover that the captain is disliked by the ship's officers and is unpopular with the crew.

Who is the finest, most adored man aboard?

The chief engineer.

The chief engineer's cabin becomes our daily social hall. Each afternoon, Rachel, Chicha, and I, together with the off-duty officers, gather there for a jolly time.

How do we communicate?

With gestures, with laughter. Some speak a little German, as we do. Jack translates in Yiddish. And everyone teaches us English.

In return we teach Hungarian, and, in fun, indulge in childish pranks.

Poor innocents that we all were!

I'm sorry, fellows, but *Sarokrád* is not really shredded sour cabbage. *Sarokrád*, in Hungarian, means, "I shit on you."

We never meant it literally, fellows. You know that. It was all in fun. You taught us words, and we taught you words. And we laughed and laughed and laughed.

We have such good times in the chief engineer's cabin. The only one not included is the captain, who, if he knows of our frolics, must be jealous—and, of course, the German woman. No one sees her, other than at eating times. After each meal she disappears below deck, where the crew and the sixteen passenger soldiers are quartered.

We are protected and looked after by everyone on the officers' deck. The officers are brothers, fathers, teachers to us. They are not lovers, although they do love us. There is only one true love story in the making—Jack and Chicha—and even Chicha herself cannot believe what is happening.

xix

I f the chief engineer's cabin is our gathering place for
fun and laughter, Jack's cabin is our refuge for tears
and comfort. After all, Jack is the only Jew besides us on
board, and we have only recently come from a poisonous,
Jew-hating world.

We were uprooted from our land of birth, banished, and
butchered. We grew up in a country where nearly everyone
who was not Jewish disliked or hated almost everyone who
was.

Why—because our people pray in a temple that bears no
cross?

At home we did have a number of friends who were
Christian. Still, they were so few, we could never feel absolutely safe.

On the S.S. *Brand Whitlock* we love all these good Christian men around us. We truly love them; they are so kind to

us. But can they understand our suffering the way Jack, the son and grandson of Jews who had suffered the pogroms of czarist Russia, can understand it? It is too soon for us not to be wary of Christians. It is natural for us to fear Gentiles and to turn more readily to a Jew for solace.

Daily, before each meal, Jack, with menu in hand, appears at our cabin. In Yiddish he explains each dish to us, so that we can later point out our choices to the waiter. It is one of Jack's most thoughtful acts, and we are so grateful.

But everything Jack does is thoughtful, from providing aspirin to listening to our sorrow. We are his family; he is ours. We have come from such horror—and have met Jack so near in time to that horror—that our relationship is being forged in a very special way.

Jack is not a survivor. He is a native American, our first Jew from the "good life"; for right now he and the ship are all the good that life can offer.

Jack is modest and somewhat shy. Sharing our sorrow and tales of hardship, he tells us of the Great Depression in America and of the hard times his family has endured with his father barely eking out a living for his wife and eight children, sometimes earning just enough for potatoes. Now his father is in some kind of trucking business and the family is managing.

Because Jack is the first person from the New World, from across the cleansing sea, to intimately touch our lives, he will always be dear to us in our life ahead. Right now, however, he is especially dear to Chicha.

How do the mysterious forces of love work? Has anyone ever found the answer?

Attraction. Chemistry. Animal magnetism. Love at first sight. Words and clichés explain nothing. Language is feeble when confronted with reality, and the reality aboard this American liberty ship at this moment is that two young strangers, each from a world entirely alien to the other, have met and have been drawn together powerfully and tenderly.

Only twenty-four hours after their first meeting at the dining room table, where Jack ordered Chicha's food for her, the two were openly seeking each other out, finding ways to saunter off together, to be together in odd corners of the vessel at odd hours of the day, to be together beneath the star-filled sky at night.

Up until now, Rachel, Chicha, and I have been a virtually inseparable trio; suddenly, Rachel and I are finding ourselves increasingly alone, wondering about the whereabouts of our sister Chicha, marveling at the exquisite miracle of it all. Later, when Chicha finally appears, she is radiant and bubbly. She cannot explain exactly where she has been or what is happening to her. Like a mechanical doll, she keeps repeating, "I'm in love. I'm in love. I'm in love."

We are told we can write to my father, telling him that we will see him soon. We don't know how our letter will reach him from the high seas, but we are happy that we can let him know we are on our way. The secrecy shrouding wartime travel and communication makes us feel like characters in some kind of international drama.

An American officer who speaks to us in German reinforces this feeling. His interest is in the German-American woman who is traveling with us. Is there anything we can tell him about her?

There is nothing we can relate; we don't know the

woman. But I do recall unexpectedly coming upon her while she was fussing with her collection of Nazi postage stamps, each bearing the likeness of *der Führer*. There she was, kissing the stamps in adoration.

May she and her beloved *Führer* rot together in purgatory!

XX

The ship has been at sea for several days. For some unknown reason, we are on a southeasterly course toward the Caucasus, rather than a southwesterly one toward the Bosporus. Later we learn that the vessel is to take on a cargo of sisal at Batumi, a Russian port at the eastern end of the Black Sea, before heading west.

Rachel and I are now accustomed to seeing the unmasked affection between Jack and Chicha. They make no attempt to hide it. We spot them lovingly holding each other, kissing in the corridors, disappearing entirely for long interludes.

A mixture of feelings invades our souls. We are delighted, worried, curious, envious. Still, we recognize that a strange healing process is at work. God, let the process work its magic around the clock. Let there be renewal. Let our fragmented lives become whole again. Let us arrive in the New World with new bodies, new hair, and new hearts, hearts that beat to the sounds of life and love, not fear.

At Batumi some of the crew are permitted to go ashore while the Russian cargo is being loaded on to the American vessel. To our surprise Jack is one of those descending the rope ladder from the S.S. *Brand Whitlock*.

Chicha cannot believe her eyes as she watches Jack disappear beyond the immediate dock area. Her newfound security, vested in Jack, suddenly seems to have vanished.

"Where's he going?" she asks Rachel and me. "Where's he going?" As though we can provide an answer and reassurance.

"He'll be back soon," we tell her. "He must have some business to attend to."

But we are equally anxious and worried, for Jack represents not only something very personal to Chicha, but also, as our translator, our vital link to everyone else on the ship. In addition, we had, even as youngsters, heard about the unreliability of sailors. They were men who had a girl in every port, or so we were told.

After what seems endless hours of on-deck vigil, watching the loading operations and the activity on the dock, we see the American seamen begin to return. Soon we see Jack. He appears to be in good humor—and a bit tipsy.

As Jack makes his way up the dangling ladder, Chicha begins to seethe. She mumbles choice Hungarian epithets. Her relief at seeing "her man" return is mixed with obvious jealousy.

At last Jack is back on board among his fellow officers, who are engaged in jocular banter. So far, he has not seen us, but as he moves along the deck toward his quarters, he suddenly discovers Chicha in his path.

"Did you enjoy the Russian women?"

Jack, not comprehending a single word, opens his arms and breaks into a broad, toothy grin. "Chicha! I missed you. I should have stayed on board."

In a single enveloping gesture, he embraces her, virtually smothering her in his arms.

The next moment, as the two stand kissing, the American officers break into laughter, hoots, and applause. Rachel and I, somewhat embarrassed, make our way back to our cabin.

Did we ever dream that we would become world travelers, see the sun sparkle on slender minarets in Istanbul, hear the bustling sounds of a Turkish port? We have sailed clear across the Black Sea, through the Bosporus Straits, and are now plowing through the Sea of Marmora. If only we could go ashore and stroll the way we strolled on the way to Odessa.

But we are not allowed to debark anywhere; only some of the crew can do so. We envy them. We are traveling freely, it seems, but in relative confinement, delicious confinement, still not free to explore strange, wondrous places. Someday, when war will not curtail our movements, we shall return.

Our curiosity is vibrantly alive. We learned about Turkey and the Bosporus and the Dardanelles when we were schoolchildren in Hungary. Now, courtesy of World War II and Adolf Hitler, here we are.

Mealtimes are somewhat formal in the dining room. The captain sets the tone, and he is stiff and pompous. We have relearned our table manners, and it is easy to eat with knife and fork leisurely, the way the English did.

There is enough glorious food on the *Brand Whitlock* to satisfy the vultures of Auschwitz. I am overfed. No one can tell that just a few months ago—in January, as a matter of fact—all of me weighed less than parts of me do now. I am actually getting fat.

It is not natural for me to be fat. I am simply stuffed, like a force-fed goose, and nothing will stop me from eating more, much more. If my face is indeed as beautiful as they say, there is a great spread of it. Let it be. I cannot imagine ever intentionally going on a diet to reduce my weight. More readily can I imagine stealing food rather than saying no to any offer.

Then there is the matter of my pride, as with Sam, the waiter, who dislikes me.

Sam and I are unable to communicate with each other, but each of us is capable of a full-blown emotional reaction, a negative one. Sam waits on the captain's table, and he never fails to subject me to an icy glance when he attends to my needs.

I don't know the source of his resentment, but I return the ice. *I don't like you either, Sam.*

Then, one day, it happens. Not being able to speak English, I point to an item on the menu simply because the spelling is similar to a Hungarian word.

"Do you know what you're ordering?" I hear Sam say with ice in his voice.

I nod, praying that the mysterious item will turn out to be a feast.

"Are you sure this is what you want, all you want?"

Bewildered, perspiring from my insecurity, I hold my ground. "Yes," I say in Hungarian. "I know what I want. *This*. This is exactly what I want."

Sam shrugs and disappears. Moments later he returns

and triumphantly places my humiliating choice, with its sour odor, in front of my nose—a heaping dish of steaming sauerkraut!

Sam, I really don't like you, nor sauerkraut. But damn it, Sam, I'm going to eat every last shred!

And I do.

Although I'm getting heavier, Rachel is not. She is seasick much of the time and cannot retain the food she so craves. Still, the security of the ship—all the love, attention, and care—keeps her spirits high. We are all the happier for the bittersweet humor that gushes out of her in Hungarian, for her Yiddish is far weaker than mine or Chicha's.

Chicha and I translate Rachel's Hungarian into Yiddish for Jack, who, in turn, translates it into English for the Americans who understand not a word of Hungarian or Yiddish but laugh even before the translation is complete. The Americans respond to us with joy because they want to see us happy. We are their family from another planet, a gift from a place called Auschwitz.

xxi

Late at night the dining room is an informal center for social life and snacks. The German woman never joins us. She doesn't belong. She is in self-appointed exile. Either she must feel very guilty, or she actually is.

The late-night snacks are a particularly warm aspect of our glorious, endless rolling on the sea. The officers come in shirtsleeves. They are relaxed and talkative, and our attempts at spoken English are more brazen and funnier than ever. Our gestures in hand-and-feet language are broad and nonsensical, but we all understand each other. We are a very happy family.

On this occasion, all attention focuses on Jack and Chicha. Accidentally, Chicha spills some water on Jack. Playfully, Jack returns the spill. Deliberately, Chicha retaliates. Swiftly, Jack splashes back. Suddenly, bedlam breaks out.

Chicha and Jack, like two combatants, grab for any water in sight. One hurls water at the other, the other hurls back. Splash for splash. Spill for spill.

In moments each is soaking wet. Tables are being shoved about. Dishes and utensils are rattling. Chairs are toppling. The men are scrambling and shouting. The floor is flooded and slippery.

Jack flees into the kitchen. In an instant he is back, pouring a pitcher of water over Chicha's head.

Chicha races into the kitchen. She returns with another pitcher.

Splash!

Jack is dripping and laughing.

Chicha is soaked and laughing.

Water is everywhere—on the tables, the chairs, the walls, the floor. The dining room is literally awash at sea.

Suddenly, the two warriors are locked in a wet, soggy embrace.

The men, now laughing uncontrollably, are standing around applauding.

Rachel and I sink into two wet chairs and go limp with joy.

Word of the water skirmish swiftly spreads through the ship, and soon we learn that the crew's late-night snack privilege has been suspended for breach of discipline.

Jack calls the punishment too severe for what he regards as a minor infraction. "It was only a harmless spat," he tells the captain. "The crew shouldn't be punished for something that is basically my fault."

"Are you in love with all three of them or only one?" the captain asks with undisguised envy over Jack's special relationship with us.

Jack ignores the question and reiterates his own responsibility.

After a day or two, with crew resentment mounting, the captain relents and restores the nighttime snack privilege. Interestingly, none of the crew's anger has been directed at Jack or us—only at the captain. Love, obviously, has emerged triumphant, for the feelings between Jack and Chicha are now more securely locked in place.

Thank you, Captain, for letting us all eat again—both day and night.

The memories of war and hatred are never far below the surface of our troubled minds, waiting to be summoned forth. Now, somewhere in the Mediterranean Sea, they break through to the surface. In the still of night, a shrill alert sounds, triggering fear and apprehension. We hear shouts and the sounds of men running in the corridor outside our cabin.

German subs!

Enemy mines!

Danger!

Following the emergency procedures we have been practicing, we rush to the deck, donning our life jackets on the way. Having been rudely awakened, I am completely disoriented and fear-ridden. Oblivious of everyone around me and terrified of freezing in the ocean, I struggle with the first piece of clothing I have grabbed while running from my cabin—a small pink undergarment.

With no ability to act or think intelligently, I try desperately to pull the tiny slip over my life jacket. The more I struggle, the less successful I am.

Suddenly, I become conscious of laughter, uncontrolled

laughter. I stop struggling and look about. The entire crew is on deck, watching me. *I* am the object of their laughter. The alert is over.

As the all-clear sounds, I flee back to my cabin in embarrassment.

The S.S. *Brand Whitlock* is gliding its way to the Algerian port of Oran.

Rachel, the talented, mothering baby in our shrunken family, is preparing for the blazing sun of North Africa. She slices up some pajamas from our "thieving" days after liberation and begins to fashion three bathing suits. There is not enough fabric to make large suits, so they turn out to be perhaps the first bikinis in the world.

We are complimented by the men with such words as "cover girls" and "glamor girls," and the names of fashion magazines are mentioned that we never heard of. The captain has three canvas chairs scrubbed bone-white; they are placed on the top deck for us, and we begin to bake our bodies under a broiling sky millions of miles, millions of years away from the broiling stench of Auschwitz.

Everything good—food, water, showers, the ability to use a bathroom—everything we have reminds us of everything we did not have just a few short months ago. A few months ago we didn't even have bodies enough to bronze under an African sun. We live by constant comparisons. It is hard enough to live in one world; we are destined to live forever in two.

The captain arranges absolute protective privacy for us. No one is to come near us while we sunbathe. Half naked, we recall our joyful childhood summers in the Carpathian Mountains. Reminiscing and dreaming of happier days, we fall asleep.

Late at night, three Hungarian sun goddesses are lobster-red, in need of care and sympathy. Jack and the captain gently touch our shoulders. Jack, in charge of first aid, provides us with a soothing ointment.

We return to the open deck to marvel at Oran, the first fully lighted city we have seen since 1939.

At Oran the ship docks briefly while a crewman is escorted ashore for medical treatment. The man has severed a finger in a machine-shop accident below decks, and there is no surgeon aboard to treat him. Soon thereafter, we are sailing away toward Gibraltar, where we are to rendezvous with a convoy of thirty or forty other ships for the transatlantic voyage to America.

The *Brand Whitlock* makes arrangements for a noontime rendezvous, and Rachel, Chicha, and I are told to be on deck. Apparently, we three young women, an extraordinary wartime cargo, are to be displayed to the disbelieving, envious eyes of the convoy.

An army of flirtatious, whistling men greets us as our ship passes into position. The men seem more than willing to swim over and transport us to their ships.

A smug, self-satisfied *Brand Whitlock* sails into the Atlantic.

We are inching our way toward a father who cannot be notified of the date of our arrival. We want to see him, but we also want to stay on the ship forever, for life has never been this good to us.

Some nights are chilly as the convoy plows through the giant waves of the ocean. Rachel is again protective and creative. She spreads out on deck the one gray blanket we hauled along, cuts it into sections, and, with needle and thread, spends our social afternoons in the chief engineer's cabin fashioning a hooded marvel of a coat that all three of us share from time to time. Somewhere, someone will have to watch over Rachel, for she never stops watching over Chicha and me.

xxii

April 12, 1945, on the high seas. We don't understand the words on the radio in the dining room. We see only the gloom around us.

Can there have been a reversal of all our fortunes? Is Hitler winning the war again? Will the world become a morgue? Is history's longest arm of evil reaching us right across the ocean?

The men listen to the radio intently. We dare not interrupt. We are afraid to learn of new catastrophes. A sorrowful cloud hangs over us. There are detectable tears.

"Jack, are there Yiddish words for the trouble?"

"Yes. President Roosevelt is dead."

Suddenly, a painful memory seizes us. Roosevelt was going to be our president, too; but we remember him also as our failed savior.

The last country to be occupied by Nazi troops was Hungary. Everyone was saying that it is up to Roosevelt to save Hungary's Jews. The war is in its final phase. Hitler is no longer as strong as he was. Perhaps now he could be negotiated with for the last remnants of European Jewry.

We don't know what actually happened to the other Jews. We know only that we are the last ones on Hitler's death list, and the teeth of the beast are not as sharp as they used to be. Maybe there is hope for us—but only if President Roosevelt comes to our aid.

Rumors fly from Hungarian town to Hungarian town. Rumors of ransoms. Rumors of exchanges. Jews for gold. Jews for trucks. All kinds of secret negotiations are said to be taking place, and the possibilities are always connected with the American president.

On March 19, 1944, the Nazi killers finally enter Hungary. But hope is still alive. Every Jewish prayer is tied to Roosevelt. Roosevelt will save us.

Why, then, are we in the cattle cars?

We share the Americans' grief, but there is a separate compartment of Jewish tragedy in our hearts that is ambivalently linked with this American president. We cry over his death and for the millions of Jewish funerals we never had. Our mourning is awash in complexities we cannot untangle. Our pain ducts open and close. With a new-found loyalty to a country we were not born in, but want to be natives of, we mourn along with the Americans.

The S.S. *Brand Whitlock* keeps chopping the waves of the Atlantic, speeding us to a reacquaintance with our father, speeding us to a land of new culture, new language, new faith in a better tomorrow. Our old luggage keeps weighing us down, imprisoning us with all we carry in our minds. We yearn to rest our cluttered heads on a new continent, separated by great waters from the cursed continent on which we were born.

We have been at sea for more than a month. It is now May 6, and we are drawing closer to the shores of the United States. Chicha, Rachel, and I huddle together in Jack's cabin.

Jack talks to us about this new world we are about to encounter: skyscrapers, buildings that rise to the clouds in New York; the world's tallest building, the Empire State; Times Square and Forty-second Street, the "crossroads of the world," where there is a blaze of lights not from a single movie house, as in Kisvarda, but from an entire block of movie houses.

He tells us about the New York Times Building and its exterior flashing news ribbon that will spell out the word *Peace* in electric lights; about the subway trains that carry millions of people underground, going or returning from places where they earn their livelihood; about trolley cars clanking in a bustling metropolis, where, through the noise, every accent, every language can be heard from every corner of the world.

He speaks of Ellis Island and New York harbor, where millions of immigrants have been greeted by a "Lady" holding high a torch of liberty; of Manhattan Island, where people can be seen wearing native clothes from far-off hamlets or designer clothes from Paris, where one can eat Jewish rye bread, Kansas beef, or Chinese delicacies.

He describes a land where the color of people's skin can vary from white to black, from yellow to red; where people can be Protestant, Baptist, Buddhist, or Catholic—even Jewish or atheist—and they all live together in that melting pot called democracy; where people ride in huge automobiles or sweat in the belly of the earth; where there are slums and estates with private tennis courts, tall Texans and short Mexicans, the very rich and the very poor, a great many people who are neither rich nor poor, just citizens of a free country, a country very different from those we have known.

We listen with rapt attention as Jack talks on and on about his country, about the country that is soon to be ours. We are eager to learn, and he "teaches" us more and more, both good and bad. He speaks of justice and injustice, of fairness and decency. He tells us of lynchings and the Ku Klux Klan, of "No Jews Allowed" country clubs and "White Only" toilets in the South. But, he assures us, there is also a constant churning for change for the better.

America is a land where hate has an air of impermanence; where women can vote and there are secret ballots; where money clanks louder than anywhere else, because there is so much of it; where even the president can be addressed as "you" or "mister"; where nothing is just right but perhaps less wrong than in almost any other place in the world. America is a land where bad can be, and often is, made better.

"You are going to an imperfect country," Jack says finally, "where your lives can be better than anytime before. There are anti-Semites everywhere; still, you will feel relatively equal."

Before we return to our quarters, Jack kisses each of us and hands us a twenty-dollar bill. "I may not be with you when we arrive," he says. "I may be on duty, but I will get in touch."

We have never seen American currency before; twenty dollars seems like a lot of money. We wonder whether he can afford it.

100

Part Four

America

xxiii

May 8, 1945. The S.S. *Brand Whitlock*, bearing the very first survivors of Auschwitz to the United States, is slipping into the harbor at Newport News, Virginia.

Cipi! Philip! The war is over!
It is V-E Day, and Hitler's war is over!
And we are in America!

We are numb. This remarkable coincidence of timing defies our ability to deal with the reality. We cannot believe that we are in the center of modern man's most momentous day. To arrive in America on the very day the war ends is too much for us to demystify. It seems entirely unlikely that any survivors of Hitler's death camps have preceded us. The importance of this soon becomes apparent: we are informed that we have an eight A.M. appointment the following morning with some American officials.

1945. Rachel, Chicha, and I are ushered to a large conference room on the ship by a middle-aged man in a military uniform. The man speaks perfect Hungarian and is one of several important-looking men with briefcases. We discover later that they are from the FBI.

The Hungarian-speaking American gently asks us about Auschwitz. Can we please tell him what we know—in detail?

We tell him about Dr. Mengele, the SS Angel of Death. We tell him about Irma Grese, his beautiful female counterpart.

After Mengele, Grese was the most feared force in our deadly lives. She was the *Oberscharführerin*, seemingly more in charge of our daily existence than anyone else. From the roots of her hair to the nails on her toes, Grese was saturated with deeds so evil and so abhorrent that the likes of her could not ever have been part of the human family.

We are calm and soft-spoken. Our tale in Hungarian sounds even more horrifying than when we tried to tell the same story in Yiddish to the English flier in Odessa. Even from this distance, I feel the terror of the time that Grese let her German shepherd loose on a helpless prisoner.

"If you make a sound," Grese warned us, "you are next."

In silent, sickening horror, we stood by and watched the German attack dog chew up the shrieking human being.

(Soon after the war, Irma Grese was one of the Nazi war criminals to be caught, tried, convicted, and hanged. I wonder whether our testimony on that May 9 was used at her trial, whether we helped in some small way to eliminate the beast.)

The morning wears on. The questions are weighing us down, but we know that the information we are conveying is important, so we summon our strength and supply the answers. Much of our memories we would like to bury at the bottom of the ocean, but some of our answers relate to happier events, such as our liberation.

Finally, the officials pack our lives into their briefcases, bid us farewell, and we rejoin our *Brand Whitlock* family.

Only hours are left of our togetherness. "Good-bye time" is upon us again. Our blessed ship is sailing the last few miles of its healing journey. We are on our way to the last stop of our twentieth-century odyssey.

It is Thursday, May 10, 1945. We anchor at a port on the Patapsco River estuary near the Chesapeake Bay. Four and a half weeks and half a world away from Odessa, Rachel, Chicha, and I leave the kindest floating haven in the world. We gingerly step onto the soil of the United States and into the American city of Baltimore, Maryland.

We leave tears and thanks with the human beings who were so good to us. Jack will contact us, he assures us in a hasty parting, on his first free day in New York. With the exception of Jack and a chance encounter with one of the ship's officers some years later, we never see any of our mentors again.

It is raining heavily in Baltimore. It is late afternoon as immigration officers guide us to a streetcar. Arrangements have been made with Judge Simon E. Sobeloff, one of Baltimore's most distinguished Jewish citizens and the future solicitor general of the United States, to be our host until our father is located.

We step on the streetcar and, for the first time in our lives, see black people. We gape, too innocent even to be embarrassed about our shock and delight. They look so beautifully suntanned, so healthy, that I wonder, almost

aloud, whether the white people around us are suffering
from consumption. In our ignorance and naïveté, and because the blacks are clustered together in one part of the
trolley, we speculate whether they all might be of the same
family. We are overwhelmed by the sudden foreignness of
everything around us.

We finally reach our destination, a large, beautiful home,
and are warmly greeted by Mrs. Sobeloff, a short, blond
bundle of loving care. Mrs. Sobeloff, a socially conscious
woman, is deeply involved with the National Council for
Jewish Women and is more than ready to assume the role of
substitute mother to three Hungarian orphans.

Shortly thereafter, Judge Sobeloff arrives with his two
friendly daughters. Immediately, instinctively, we know
that the Sobeloffs have adopted us for lifelong friendship.

While we dine in unaccustomed elegance, Judge Sobeloff
makes an exhausting series of phone calls to find our father
in New York. Intermittently, he asks us in Yiddish for bits
of information that may aid his search.

There is no M. Katz listed at the address we provide;
there is no M. Katz anywhere near that address. Also, there
are many Katzes in New York, but none who is our father.

After a great deal of struggle with telephone operators
and their supervisors, Judge Sobeloff reaches a resident at
the first address we gave him.

"Is there a man named M. Katz living in your building?
This is very important."

"I have a neighbor whose brother is living with her. His
name is Katz, but I don't know if he's the man you want."

"Would you please be kind enough to get him? His children are looking for him."

After a long interval a voice responds in Hungarian.

I take the receiver and listen. The voice belongs to my

aunt, who emigrated to America when I was just a child. I vaguely remember what she looks like but little else. She is talking to me rapidly in her native tongue.

"Yes, we know you're alive. A letter fell out of my daughter's schoolbook telling us you were on your way."

I wonder how the letter got there. It is too mysterious.

"Your father's not here. He's in temple. He's praying. He prays all the time. We'll find him. Give us your number. You'll hear from us soon. Thank God you're alive."

At Simon Sobeloff's home we all sit vigil, waiting. It is late when the phone finally rings. My father is weeping at the other end.

We have no answers to his questions. We are frightened, bewildered. What can we say to him? We recognize his voice but can't believe we have a parent.

We know that he cannot immediately come to us because of the closeness of the Sabbath. We are prepared for what he tells us—immediately after the Sabbath he will board a train and be with us early Sunday morning.

He blesses our hosts and promises to take care of everything when he sees us. He will have papers and will reimburse the government for our passage. He will spend the Sabbath praying for the safe arrival of the rest of his family.

For two days we try not to think about what to tell my father. It is easy and pleasant to be with the Sobeloffs. We do not share family tragedy with them. With my father it will be different.

We are cared for with tenderness and kindness. We keep finding new families but cannot put ours together. The first thing we'll do in New York is place an ad in a paper:

"Has anyone seen Cipi or Philip?"

xxiv

In anticipation of our father's arrival, breakfast is served
very early Sunday morning at the Sobeloff home. The
sweets taste sour. The sour tastes sweet. The chaos in our
emotions affects even our taste buds.

We are afraid of the impending meeting. Whoever the
bureaucrats were in Washington throughout the war years,
they did not issue the necessary documents to our father
with urgent dispatch so that he could save his family before
Hitler devoured them. The bureaucrats played the game of
red tape, of rules and regulations, up to the last hideous
moment.

If the bureaucrats had let our father bring his family to
the United States without the hocus-pocus of immigration
papers, then Dr. Mengele would have been cheated of the
pleasure of sending one more Jewish family to the ovens. In
the face of such deadly danger, should that have not been

reason enough to bypass the insanity of bureaucratic paper-pushing? After all, our father was a legal resident of the United States, having resided in the country for years, and just a bit of time away from full citizenship.

And now our father is going to be here within the hour, and he will ask us, "Where is Mother? Where is Cipi? Where is Potyo, my youngest child? Where is Philip, my only son, my *Kaddish*?"

"Father, Father," we will say, "they are on their way."

We will lie and lie. We will not tell him the truth. We cannot bear the truth. We hate ourselves. We hate the whole world.

We are standing in the Sobeloff living room, hugging, weeping, and lying to an aging man. We have found a father, and it is inherent in the larger tragedy that we have also lost him.

There is a profound, instant aura of alienation between us. There are long moments of silence. Our father was in agony for years, but he was in agony in America. We were in agony in Auschwitz.

The gap is too wide. How can we transmit the scent, the smoke, the pall of Auschwitz? The countless dead will all narrow down to two charred bodies, mother and Potyo. Our father will not be able to accept this kind of truth, and we will not force it down his wounded throat.

The Sobeloff living room is awash with all that Hitler wrought.

XXV

For all his years, my father kept his faith with the man in the heavens. If the entrance to the heavens is the sky, the sky has been brutalized. It lost its color of blue when Dr. Mengele painted it weeping gray. The fire leaping toward the heavens was kept aglow with the bodies of our mothers, our children.

What is my father to do with his servitude to God? Take Him to task? Perhaps, my father says, we have all been punished for sinning against the Almighty.

My father turns more fanatically religious than ever.

We are now living in a spacious apartment, after a brief sojourn at my aunt's house. At first my father tiptoes around us with pleas for godliness, then he grows more demanding. He wants us to live a life of total devotion. He tries to literally bribe us into believing in the mercy of God.

All we want to do is live, Father. We cannot solve your

quarrel with your God. Our brains are too worn for the battle, Father. Let us be.

Newspaper, radio, and film people seek us out. They want to interview us, the first Auschwitz survivors in America, to see if we are real.

My father bars the door to all of them. We are grateful for that. Then, in earnest, people from all over the country begin to flock to our house.

"Have you seen my mother? Her name was Sarah."

"Have you seen my father, my sisters?"

"We come from Munkacs . . . from Beregszaz . . . from Nyireghyhaza. Have you seen my brother? What happened to my family? When do you think they'll be coming? How lucky you are to be the first to come."

What do these people want from us? Don't they know what happened?

They are all beggars. They want us to give them something that no longer exists—their families. They want us to give them their Sarahs and Yankeles and Rivkalas, and they are no more. They are practically forcing us to give them a crumb of hope.

But we are not in the business of providing impossible hope. The hope we have, we need to live on. We cannot squander it on lies.

Ask Dr. Mengele. He knows. He must be living somewhere in luxury. He was the almighty in Auschwitz. He had the power over the lives of all these people you are asking us to remember.

We remember no one. There is no one.

The door bell rings. There is a uniformed man at the door. It is Jack.

"Father, this is the good man we spoke to you about.

112

This is the man who was thoughtful enough to give us money when we disembarked from the *Brand Whitlock*.

"Father, he was so good to us. His name is Jack, and we owe him twenty dollars."

"I am grateful to the officer and will return his money. But not today. Today is the Sabbath, and we do not handle money on the Sabbath."

Silly Jack! How could you? We told you about our father. We told you how religious he was. Couldn't you have come tomorrow?

Poor Chicha is aching to embrace and kiss her love, but she must pretend that he is merely a friend. We must all pretend.

Jack will never do for my father. He is not religious; he is practically a *goy*, a Gentile. He rang the door bell on the Sabbath. He probably came by taxi.

Jack doesn't want to leave. He just sits there, in love, silent, bewildered, afraid to step on anyone's holy toes.

We all sit there. We all look dumb. Everyone is uncomfortable.

The officer has been sitting there too long. What does he want?

There is no suspicion yet, but a germ of it is growing.

Finally, Jack slips a telephone number to Chicha and leaves.

Everything is Hitler's fault. Everything is due to the war. If my mother were alive, she would smooth things, as she always did. She would negotiate my father's unreasonable demands.

My father hugs me. He pleads with me to go to temple.

"Go upstairs where the women are. Pray for your mother. Pray for the dead."

But the dead didn't just die, Father. They were murdered! I am not grateful for that, Father. My lips freeze in temple. I cannot praise the Lord. I am trying so hard to live with the clutter in my head. Let me be.

Live the way you can, Father. Let me live the way I can. Please.

xxvi

P hilip is alive.
A letter has arrived from an American soldier, Private First Class Berent: "We liberated your son. He is in a hospital. He tried to escape and the Nazis shot him. He is not seriously injured. He is fine. He'll be perfectly all right."

Should I go to temple?

My father is there now.

It will take several months before Philip can be with us, but we can make peace with the waiting period. All we wanted to know was that he was alive, in good enough condition to repair whatever damage he sustained.

Philip, do you know anything about Cipi?

We place an ad in the Hungarian-language newspaper begging anyone with knowledge of Cipi to get in touch with us.

No one responds.

We cry in Hitler's wilderness.

"If it isn't asking too much," writes my father to Private First Class Berent, "could you please write another brief letter concerning the whereabouts of my son. Is he still in the hospital?

"I have sent letters to my friends in Switzerland, England, and France, instructing them to care for my son, if possible. I will bring him to New York from any one of those countries.

"Also, please tell my son to pursue his religion as befits a Jewish boy like him. Please aid my son in any way. I will reimburse you immediately for any expenses.

"Enclosed is a money order for my son, Philip.

"Sending you and my son my everlasting love, I remain yours, M. Katz.

"P.S. If possible, please ask my son to write a letter in his own handwriting."

Philip's survival strengthens and reaffirms my father's faith. Rachel, Chicha, and I are deeply religious in our love for our brother—and for our father—but we cannot come to terms with the countless dead.

My father suffers. He cannot compromise the way he lives. And we suffer. We are not asking him to abandon his faith. We just cannot live his way. Our minds are hardly clear about anything. We know only that the mountain in front of our vision is too mammoth.

My father's questions about my mother's arrival become less frequent. We wonder how much he knows. We never spell out details, to him or anyone. The "ugly thing" sits inside us, sealed, as in an iron box.

We had to speak about it in Odessa and on the ship, but from here on, we may not be able to talk about it for decades, perhaps ever.

From here on, we shall just try to live.

xxvii

C hicha uses a public telephone to call Jack at the number he gave her. She tells him that we have a live brother. Jack loves the news. He loves Chicha. They agree to meet secretly on a street corner, Delancey and Essex.

They meet the next day, and the next, and the next. No one sees them until an uncle accidentally encounters them on the subway. The uncle rushes to inform my father, whose suspicion is now confirmed—the *goy* in uniform is more than a friend.

My father is in a quandary. Till now, all his dreams and plans for his family have been shattered. First by Hitler and his henchmen, then by Roosevelt and his bureaucrats. Through it all, however, he has maintained his faith in his God.

He has prayed and practiced his religion with pious devotion. He has not questioned the nature or the will of the Almighty. He has sacrificed and mourned in his fashion. Throughout the years of separation from his family, he has lived on a Spartan diet, forgoing his favorite foods as a symbolic identification with his hungry and oppressed people. His handsome, tailored suits he hung in the darkest recesses of his closet, where they remained unworn, growing stale with disuse, a self-imposed deprivation.

And God, in His mysterious manner, had blessed him by returning three daughters to his hearth and by saving his only son, who ultimately would say *Kaddish*, the holy prayer for the dead, when in good time the Lord would call his son's aged father to His fold.

Now, once again, ungodly forces and man-made circumstances were conspiring to threaten the proper and holy order of his destiny. His daughter Chicha was in imminent danger. A stranger, an alien, beardless, nondevotional "Jew" was luring his child away from her heritage.

What could he do to separate and keep this goy, this Jack, from his divinely returned daughter, the direct descendant of holy rabbis?

At first he cajoles, pleads, and reasons. He invokes the name of God, the blessings of God, the wrath of God. Calamity upon calamity has befallen those who have departed from the paths of righteousness, the way of the Book, the customs of their people. A Jewish maiden must pursue the sacred path of her forebears. She must seek a mate in accordance with divine dictates and with paternal approval. She must honor and respect the will of her father.

But an abyss, neither of my father's making nor of ours, has opened between us. A force that is ungoverned by reason, by logic, by ancestral practice has taken control of the souls of the participants in this Hitler-created drama.

118

Chicha and Jack, who can communicate verbally with each other only through an elementary command of the Yiddish language, have nevertheless been drawn together through a silent, voiceless communication that transcends such barriers as mere words. This type of communication recognizes no abysses, no gulfs, no dictums. It bridges them all, and Chicha and Jack are determined to cross that bridge together. My father must recognize that this, too, is the will of God.

I am taken to visit the second of my three aunts, my father's sisters, who also live in New York. I am not averse to staying with this aunt for several days. She is kind and warmhearted. But I begin to miss my sisters. I cannot understand why they don't call me.

I call the neighbor with the telephone at my father's address and leave word for my sisters to contact me. They don't. I hear not a word from them. What is going on?

I begin to feel insecure. I feel isolated and deserted. I call again. They still do not respond. The enigma is tearing me apart.

I don't know my way around this huge metropolis called New York. I don't know anything about subways. My aunt's phone is silent. I can no longer endure my anxiety.

I pack my bags, kiss my aunt, and run for a taxi. I hand the driver the slip of paper with my father's address and listen to the racing of my heart.

When the taxi arrives, I run to the room my sisters and I have been sharing. Rachel and Chicha are in bed, undressed.

"We couldn't call you because they took away our clothes."

Chicha is fuming. "They don't want me to see Jack," she says, "but soon I'm going to meet him like this."

"I gave them my clothes, too," says Rachel. "If Chicha can't go out," I told them, "I don't want to go out, either."

"Here, put these on." I hand them some clothes from my bag, and they swiftly dress. Moments later the three of us are on our way to the aunt I just left. This aunt, at least, is sympathetic to our plight.

At a public phone, Chicha calls Jack and arranges to meet him just once more—to say good-bye. Everything has become much too difficult.

Jack gives her a relative's address, and we place her in a cab. We inform my aunt that Chicha has gone to tell Jack that she can never see him again.

Later, Chicha calls to say that Jack's relative has invited her to stay overnight. It is very difficult to separate forever. We simply must understand. We do.

The following day, Jack, Chicha, and Jack's youngest brother spend the hours in urgent activity. Jack is still in service; therefore, he can get a premarital blood test right away. He does, and the three "conspirators" hurry to the Lower East Side, a predominantly Jewish neighborhood, to find a rabbi holy enough to satisfy even my fanatically religious father.

They find just such a rabbi but then discover that they also need a *minyan*, ten Jewish men, to be present during the sacred rites of a Jewish ceremony. The *minyan* is not an absolute necessity, but having one will add an extra measure of orthodoxy to the marriage.

Jack and his brother race down the street and, at random, round up ten religious-looking Jews. They have their *minyan*.

Jack has purchased a wedding band. Chicha is wearing a

borrowed dress. The *minyan* is standing by. And the rabbi performs the ceremony.

The day is June 7, 1945, exactly thirty days after our arrival in the United States.

In Brookline, Massachusetts, Jack introduces his bride to his parents and the other members of his family.

Chicha is dumbfounded.

Jack, the merchant seaman she married, is not a poor American at all. He is, in fact, the son of a very wealthy man!

May you live in peace forever, Romeo of the Seas, Juliet of Auschwitz.

Part Five

Cipi and Philip

xxviii

Years have passed. Each of us is married. And we all have brought forth new life—beautiful, intelligent children.

I *know* that Cipi is dead. Still, I never stop looking.

The lady serving me in the bakery strongly resembles someone I knew. *It cannot be Cipi.* But would it hurt to ask whether she is Hungarian?

On the street, I pursue a lady whose walk resembles Cipi's. I follow her for a couple of blocks, futilely.

It is crazy, but decades later, a few survivors of the Holocaust, I hear, have met kin who were believed to have been murdered by the Nazis. I don't know such cases, but I am told that such miracles have happened. So I look. I always look.

Then something happens.

In 1978, a friend invites me to a gathering of Hungarian survivors. I rarely go to such events, but this time I do.

"Where are you from?" a stranger inquires.

"Kisvarda," I respond.

"Next door to my wife's hometown."

"What's her name?"

"Eva . . . Eva Fülöp." And he presents his wife to me.

"Oh, my God! Eva! Eva! Eva!"

We hug and kiss and weep. We cannot stop. The last time we saw each other was on the infamous winter death march in Germany, January 23, 1945, the day Chicha, Rachel, and I escaped, the day we lost Cipi.

Eva is one of six beautiful sisters who suffered with us in Auschwitz and Birnbaumel. We were inseparable; we had to be. During *Zeilappell*, *Wurstappell*, whatever *Appell*, all the prisoners had to line up in rows of five; and to be in a row of five was always the responsibility of the individual prisoners.

Whenever five prisoners got together, it was with the hope that they would form a lasting quintet. Almost always, the hope was thwarted. Some prisoners were taken on work transport; some went to the crematorium; some simply died and disappeared.

To secure a row of five was a never-ending struggle. Only Eva's family and my family were relatively secure. My family of four sisters were short one prisoner for the required five; Eva's family of six had one too many. Together we constituted two rows of five. We couldn't let each other out of sight. Our relationship was full of love, dissonance, and absolute dependence on one another. Miraculously, Eva and all her sisters survived.

"Eva, tell me what happened to Cipi. You know. So please tell me."

Eva begins the story. And I begin to weep. I cry such bitter tears that Eva stops. She refuses to say another word.

In 1980, two years later, I am ready to hear the tale. On a quiet Sunday afternoon, sitting in my secure kitchen, I steel myself and call Eva.

"Listen carefully, Eva. You are not facing me now. You cannot see me. Please tell me exactly what happened to Cipi. I promise not to cry."

"All right. I will tell you. . . . After you and Chicha and Rachel ran from the column, Cipi started after you. But it was too late. You three got away, but the SS caught Cipi.

"They dragged her back to the column and began to beat her with their rifle butts. They beat and beat and beat her.

"We, too, planned to escape, but when we saw what they did to Cipi, we decided to wait. We weren't brave. We just marched on with the column.

"Cipi was in tragic shape, so we adopted her. We shielded her as if she were our sister. We told her to do whatever we did, to be one of us. We pleaded with her, begged her to try to escape with us.

"But she was in a deep depression. She rejected all our efforts to save her. She shook her head or was totally unresponsive.

"She kept begging the SS to shoot her, but because this was what she wanted, they refused. They knew that her sisters had escaped, and her suffering could be greater by keeping her alive.

"You know how it was. You couldn't die when you wanted to die—only when the SS wanted you dead.

"Finally, we escaped. But Cipi remained on the march. She was too weak and too frightened to try again. We found out later from someone that she actually reached Bergen-Belsen, where she was liberated by the British.

"Then she died."

xxix

Philip has never talked about his experiences after he was taken as a slave laborer by the SS from Auschwitz. The most he ever said was that he had been in six concentration camps—and he had survived.

Then, one wintry day, during a wide-ranging conversation in his home, he suddenly began to talk about his final days as a prisoner of the Nazis. In essence, this is what he said:

The Nazis were in full retreat on all fronts. The Russians were closing in from the east, and the Allies were advancing from the west. But the Germans were still fighting, and though they were losing, they were determined to kill as many Jews as possible before they surrendered.

To fulfill this murderous objective, they were transporting about

129

four thousand of us, in their usual cattle cars, to some unknown killing ground.

I probably weighed no more than a child at the time and had no more than a few hours of life left in me. I was very ill and very weak. But I made one last desperate effort to survive.

We had not eaten for days. There was no food on the train, not even for the Nazis. And every few miles, the train was forced to stop because of bombing from the air.

Each time the bombs fell, we had to leave the cattle cars and lie down on the ground a short distance from the train. And each time this happened, a few SS, and one or two civilian trainmen, would desert and disappear into the woods. This told us that our liberators must be very close at hand.

With some trepidation, a Czech prisoner and I decide to gamble on a deal with the SS man in charge of us. We know we cannot trust him—he can kill us just for speaking to him—but we also know that he must be scared because the Allies are so close. If we can gain some time—an hour or two—perhaps we can be liberated by the Allied troops, whose guns we can hear in the distance.

Suppressing our fear, we approach the SS. "If you don't move us," we tell him, "we will tell the Americans that you treated us well when they get here."

The SS is taken aback by our audacity, but he doesn't shoot us. "My duty is to take you to your destination," he says.

"But it's all over. You can hear the American guns. You can save us, and we can save you."

"I don't need your saving." He raises his gun. "Now you'd better be quiet."

Sensing his lack of assurance, we abandon all caution. "The Americans will kill you, or we will kill you," we threaten. It is an incredibly laughable situation—two emaciated skeletons threatening an armed, but frightened, SS man. Finally, as the rumble of guns grows louder, we reach a tacit agreement. The SS will not force us back on the train, and we will do what we can for him.

Suddenly, the SS man says, "You know I wouldn't kill you. Don't you?" He begins to look intimidated and scared. His arrogance, which till now masked his underlying cowardice, is totally gone.

Still, I cannot trust what he says. The Germans, in the past, have been too deceitful. After all his promises, the SS man could easily turn and mow us down. So I ask permission to go to the woods to urinate, hoping to get as far from him as possible.

Just inside the woods, I find another SS deserter hastily changing his uniform for civilian attire.

Startled by my catching him in the act, he deliberately shoots me in the leg. Moments later, the cattle cars are captured by the Allies.

Amid the wild sounds of liberation, and before I fall unconscious, I see a group of female prisoners pounce on their SS guard. They trample, kick, bite, and tear her apart.

When next I open my eyes, I'm in an American hospital, and Private Berent is at my bedside asking who I am. I tell him, and then I ask a favor.

Write to my father, please. Write and tell him I'm alive.